Hi, I'm Casian Anton

I'm glad that you have decided to buy this book available for charity. This edition was printed for private readers to find error and help me to improve the final edition. The content available here is slightly different from the content available in the final edition.

I wish you a bright journey and thank you for taking the time to read this research book.

Kind regards
Casian Anton

DAY DAY UP!

August 18, 2023

CASIAN ANTON (born July 30, 1988) private analyst in International Relations with concerns in the study of interdisciplinary methodology, world state and structures of explanation. QTS in Humanities (2016 in England, 2011 in Romania, Petru Maior's University of Târgu Mureș), MA in *Security and International Relations* ('Lucian Blaga' University of Sibiu, Romania, 2013), BA in *International Relations and European Studies* (Petru Maior's University of Târgu Mureș, Romania, 2011), Erasmus Student to *University of Social Science and Humanities* (Warsaw, Poland, 2012-2013).

Author: Casian Anton
Cover: created inside the app Adobe Express (standard license)
Translated into English: Casian Anton
Series: *Papers about the World State*

Printed by Amazon

© 2022 CASIAN ANTON via Revi Project 88

"The Goals *of* World State" Black and White Edition

ISBN: 9798846836273

Revi Project 88 (London, UK): *is dedicated to create knowledge and advance the understanding of various topics in the field of Social Science & Humanities (International Relations as a specific area of study). All the activities within this project is to guide, exchange, sustain and share unique and original ideas that can help people to understand the world.*

Online orders: www.amazon.com
Contact: www.reviproject88.com
Social Media: Revi Project 88 (Twitter, Facebook, Instagram, Tumblr)

FIRST PRINTED EDITION

TO EARTH CITIZENS:

"Love is the name"
"Unus pro omnibus, omnes pro uno"

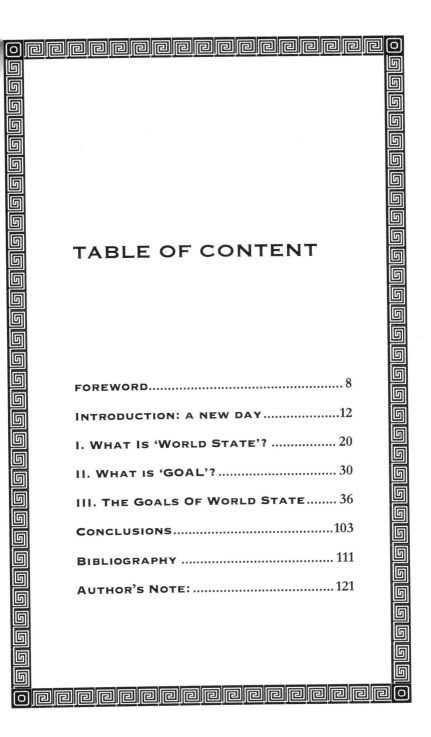

TABLE OF CONTENT

FOREWORD

1. In December 2015, in Romania, I was able to publish the first research in the Series *Papers about the World State*. In October 2022, I live in England and I have the pleasure of publishing the third and final edition where I fixed minor parts and added small changes in tone, structure and examples; these useful interventions created a version more adequate and with a better overview of the positive goals of the world state.

2. Through this research paper, I invite the Earth citizens to read another face of the world state, a subject too much marginalized in the current reality of a violent context; currently, international governmental and non-governmental organizations are not on the list of the population's preferences and fail to achieve their proposed goals, one reason being too much control of powerful and rich states in making decisions on the organization's long-term orientation and that the national interest is much more important than world interest. I'm aware that the present approach may be considered exaggerated, it may be out of touch with reality and almost impossible to achieve, but nevertheless I wanted to extend the thread of the world state narrative and research, and to present a more suitable understanding on how we should think and in which direction we should work together.

3. From December 2015 to October 2022 I experienced a major change. In February 2016 I finished my first life, and I got the chance to start my second life. Maybe humans really do have multiple lives too. In November 2016 I arrived in England where I planned a short trip of seven weeks, and in October 2022 I still live here; the name of the new city starts with letter **L**, like the first letter of the name of the village where I lived in Romania. Maybe destiny is already written in the stars and I travelled where I was supposed to go. In England I found and live the diverse, rich, difficult, *vivid and colourful* cultural environment that I wrote about in the first edition of this research; in 2015 (and today) I believed in my ideas, probably too much, but I didn't believe and see myself walking on the streets of London, tasting ice cream on a bench in Kensington Park, or riding a bike on the banks of the

River Thames, around the London Eye and the Buckingham Palace.

4. In the last research papers,[1] I did not mention any person who was involved through various discussions that helped me to acquire a greater understanding of the methods of writing and delivery of ideas. Now and here is the best time to fix the narrative where communicating ideas with friends is the bridge to success. Therefore, my thanks begin with Paul who was the first witness to the first version of the papers published in August 2021 and 2022: he participated in many discussions that appeared out of the blue when I had no better topic to deliver, and I thought that maybe it's better to confess my interests to him; I don't know if he liked it every time, but I know *for sure* that sometimes he got up from his chair and decided to leave the room, then came back later with another idea. To Andrei for the suggestions sent regarding the front cover of this paper and the text on these pages; to Maria for being interested in my research for at least ten years and reading it every time. Finally, to my family, and especially to my mother for

---

[1] Casian Anton, *Black and White Music: A Journey Behind the Musical Notes* (August 2022, iTunes, Google Play, Kobo, Smashwords, Amazon: printed version), *On the Famous Feud* (August 2022, iTunes, Google Play, Kobo, Smashwords, Amazon: printed version).

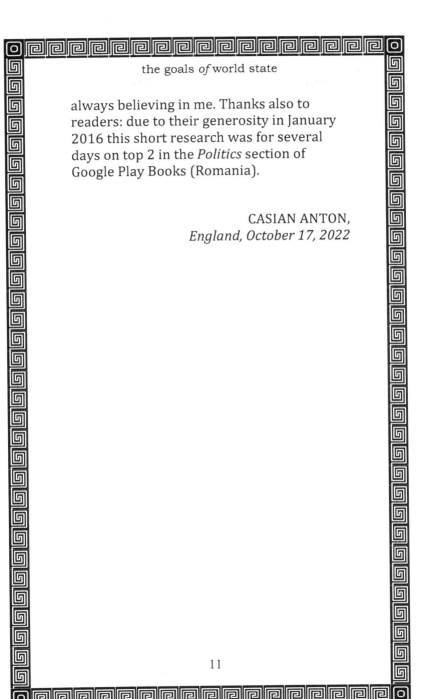

always believing in me. Thanks also to readers: due to their generosity in January 2016 this short research was for several days on top 2 in the *Politics* section of Google Play Books (Romania).

CASIAN ANTON,
England, October 17, 2022

Introduction: a new day

1. Among the Earth's inhabitants there is a strongly convinced minority that a totalitarian world state is being secretly built. The most common negative goals associated with the totalitarian world state are: **(I)** population reduction; **(II)** the destruction of nations' sovereignty and national identity; **(III)** mind and population control; **(IV)** the destruction of Christianity and its replacement by the New Age religion; **(V)** the end of democracy and individual freedom; **(VI)** mass surveillance; **(VII)** the destruction of the traditional family; **(VIII)** the world state will be organized according to the principles and rules of the constitution of Masonic lodges and governed by Masons and Jews.[2]

---

[2] See for example: John Coleman, "21 Goals of the Illuminati and The Committee of 300," *Educate-Yourself*, last accessed December 23, 2015, http://educate-yourself.org/cn/johncolemangoalsofIlluminati.shtml; Stephen Lendman, "The True Story of the Bilderberg Group

2. The sources of these negative goals are multiple and generally include stories, tv series and science-fiction films, newspaper articles and websites with known and unknown authors. The peak period of the propaganda of the negative goals was reached after the year 2000 when the Internet was available in the homes of hundreds of millions of people, then, a decade later, in the homes of over a billion people.

3. As of today, the world state is one of the most negative ideas in the world. There is a noticeable number of users on social media (eg Reddit and Twitter) who believe that the world state is the monstrosity that we must fight against by all means available. We have reached a nefarious situation: the negativists, anti-globalists, nationalists and fundamentalists accuse the pro-world state

and What They May Be Planning Now. A Review of Daniel Estulin's book," *Global Research*, last accessed December 3, 2015, http://www.globalresearch.ca/the-true-story-of-the-bilderberg-group-and-what-they-may-be-planning-now/13808; Melvin Sickler "A Satanic Plot for a One World Government: The World Conspirators: the Illuminati," *The Forbidden Knowledge*, last accessed November 27, 2015, http://www.theforbiddenknowledge.com/hardtruth/satanic_plot_government.htm; Ken Adachi, "The New World Order (NWO). An Overview," *The Forbidden Knowledge*, last accessed November 27, 2015, http://educate-yourself.org/nwo/.

activists of (I) lack of patriotism; (II) label them as traitors to the country and nation; (III) threatens them with death; (IV) request the government to revoke their citizenship; (V) promotes the idea of being exiled from the country; (VI) support with a burning passion the application of corporal punishments existing in the medieval era. And we have to admit, that as far as the totalitarian world state is concerned, there is a truth. Theorists openly admit in multiple research papers that there is a fear that the world state, once it exists, could take the form of a totalitarian world state.[3]

---

[3] See for example: Alexander Wendt, "Why a World State is Inevitable?," *European Journal of International Relations* 9 (2003): 527, accessed April 30, 2014, doi: 10.1177/135406610394001; Campbell Craig, "The Resurgent Idea of World Government," *Ethics & International Affairs* 22 (2008):142, accessed February 10, 2015, doi: 10.1111/j.1747-7093.2008.00139.x; Shmuel Nili, "Who's Afraid of a World State? A Global Sovereign and the Statist-Cosmopolitan Debate," *Critical Review of International Social and Political Philosophy* 18 (2015): 247, accessed September 9, 2015, doi: 10.1080/13698230.2013.850833; Mathias Koenig-Archibugi, "Is Global Democracy Possible?," *European Journal of International Relations* 17 (2010): 520, accessed May 19, 2014, doi: 10.1177/1354066110366056; James A. Yunker, "Evolutionary World Government," *Peace Research. The Canadian Journal of Peace and Conflict Studies* 44 (2012): 96, accessed September 3, 2015; Ronald Tinnevelt, "Federal World Government: The Road to Peace and Justice?," *Cooperation and Conflict* 47 (2012): 222-223, accessed May 19, 2014, doi: 10.1177/0010836712443173.

4. In this research paper, I decided to go against the negative thread of the world state and **(I)** I challenge the conventional wisdom of the negative goals of the world state by exploring fifty positive goals; **(II)** I help to improve the human imagination regarding the possibility of a positive end of the world state; **(III)** I invite people to believe that the world state is good for humanity as quickly as they think it is bad for humanity; **(IV)** I provide a point of reference for curious readers looking for positive goals of the world state.

4.1 The main argument of the paper is the need for a positive position to counterbalance the negative goals by building what is missing: **(I)** a narrative line where the world state can bring advantages and benefits to humanity and **(II)** creating a balance of the narrative line of the goals of the world state by adding positive ones.

5. As research methods, I used **(I)** the following questions: what could be the positive aims of the world state? Why do we need a world state? What benefits could the world state bring to the entire population of the Earth? What are the problems of today that can only be solved in a world state? Why should the people of Earth want a world state? What are the general desires of humanity?; **(II)** I have looked for positive

goals of the world state in multiple research papers; **(III)** I initiated a mental exercise, that is, I tried to answer the above questions with the help of the knowledge I had before and after reading more about the negative and positive goals of the world state.

6. After going through the bibliographic sources used in this paper, I reached the following conclusions:

(I) there is an imbalance of the goals of the world state because:

(I.I) the negative goals are few, but intensively promoted in the cyber and public space;

(I.II) the positive goals are many, but are scattered in papers in various scientific journals and books that citizens do not read:

(I.II.I) because they are pleased with the negative goals, they close themselves to any positive discussion;

(I.II.II) due to lack of access to literature about the world state, in the sense that there are no libraries or the literature is written in a foreign language that the readers do not know (most sources are in English);

16

(I.II.III) due to high prices of books and scientific articles that the readers cannot afford (a research article (10-20 pages) available on Cambridge Journals is 20£);

(I.II.IV) even if the readers go through research papers whose title includes the combination of the terms 'world state', 'global state', 'world government' or 'global government', the research paper writes between two to four positive goals, sometimes the same goals in several research papers, or write nothing about positive or negative goals;

(I.II.V) there is an unusual attraction to the negative approach of the world state: readers are much more willing to believe and accept the negative version published online; in most cases, unauthored or pseudonymous articles are more widespread than articles with the name of a real author whose existence can be verified at any time;

(II) from the research concluded, i.e. on Google, book sites and in scientific databases[4], positive goals have been written

---

[4] On Google, Amazon, Barnes and Noble, Smashwords, Kobo, iTunes, Scribd, Goodreads, CEEOL, EBSCO, ProQuest Central, Web of Science, JSTOR I searched in Romanian language: 'scopurile statului mondial,' 'scopurile statului global,' 'scopurile guvernului mondial,' 'scopurile guvernului

17

worldwide in other papers, but there is no work that brings together and explores *in-extenso* the positive goals of the world state; nor is there any research paper with the titles *The Goals of World State* or other titles such as: *The Goals of the Global State*, *The Goals of the World Government*, or *The Goals of the Global Government*.

7. The research paper is organized as follows: in chapter *I. WHAT IS 'WORLD STATE'?* I explored the multiple meanings of the concept, the changes that the world state will bring, the preservation of the existing elements in today's countries and the equal relationship of the terms used to define the world state; in chapter *II. WHAT IS 'GOALS'?*, I have defined the deceptive nature of the concept, the types and the sources of the goals of the world state; in chapter *III. THE GOALS OF WORLD STATE* I set forth the general and particular level of the positive goals of the world state; I described eight clarifications, presented and expanded fifty positive goals of the world state that together create a balance of the narrative line of the end of the state world. In *CONCLUSIONS* I returned to the main argument of the paper and the four

---

global;' and in English language: 'the goals of world state,' 'the goals of global state,' 'the goals of world government' and 'the goals of global government.'

reasons that encourage me to advance a positive research of the world state. I ended the paper with a proposal and a question for all citizens of the planet.

I. WHAT IS 'WORLD STATE'?

1. The world state is one of the most controversial topics in the world. The idea is old and has been approached by many people, for example by the most influential philosophers and researchers in the social and political science of the world (Dante Alighieri, Immanuel Kant, Hans J. Morgenthau, Alexander Wendt); by lawyers, physicists, journalists, novelists and ordinary people.[5]

---

[5] Dante Aligieri, *The Banquet,* (*Il Convito - Italian*), (1304-1306), accessed November 3, 2015, http://www.gutenberg.org/ebooks/12867, electronic edition; *De Monarchia*, 1309-1913, accessed November 3, 2015, http://oll.libertyfund.org/titles/2196, electronic edition; Immanuel Kant, *Idea for a Universal History with a Cosmopolitan Purpose*, (1784), accessed November 3, 2015, https://www.marxists.org/reference/subject/ethics/kant/u niversal-history.htm, electronic edition; *Perpetual Peace, (1795)*, accessed November 3, 2015, http://oll.libertyfund.org/titles/357, electronic edition; Hans J. Morgenthau, *Politica între naţiuni. Lupta pentru putere şi lupta pentru pace,* traducere Oana Andreea Bosoi,

2. One of the most difficult tasks of a researcher in any field is to define the concept that is used to start the discussion and the investigation for a specific research topic. This observation is also valid for the definition of the concept of 'world state': it is not universally accepted. Since in the paper I explored the goals of the 'world state', the conceptual approach scratches the surface of the research, enough to get a picture of what 'world state' is.

3. Throughout history many scholars have been involved in the definition of 'world state'. A widely shared concept among scholars is the following: "world state is a

Alina Andreea Dragolea, Mihai Vladimir Zodian (Iaşi: Editura Polirom, 2006): 517-551.

Alexander Wendt, "Why a World State is Inevitable?"; For the history of the idea of 'world state' see: Robert L. Carneiro, "The Political Unification of the World: Whether, When, and How - Some Speculations," *Cross-Cultural Research* 38 (2004): 163-169, accessed September 3, 2015, doi: 10.1177/1069397103260530; Campbell Craig, "The Resurgent Idea of World Government," *Ethics & International Affairs* 22 (2008):133; Thomas G. Weiss, "What Happened to the Idea of World Government," *International Studies Quarterly* 53 (2009): 259-262, accessed February 10, 2015, doi: 10.1111/j.1468-2478.2009.00533.x, see https://www.worldfederalistscanada.org/documents/09TW eissreWrldGovt.pdf; Luis Cabrera, "World Government: Renewed Debate, Persistent Challenges," *European Journal of International Relations* 16 (2010): 512-513, accessed May 19, 2014, doi: 10.1177/1354066109346888.

single legislative, executive and judicial authority for all the people from planet Earth, regardless of race, culture, gender, language, religion, sexual orientation." Other definitions are given below:

(I) „world government means government for and over the world;"[6]

(II) „all humankind united under one common political authority;"[7]

(III) „a legitimate authoritative organised power governing the world."[8]

There are also sentences that, extracted from a text, can be considered a concept of world state. Here are two examples:

(IV) „One World is a geographic, biological, and technological fact;"[9]

---

[6] Thomas I. Cook, "Theoretical Foundations of World Government," *The Review of Politics* 12 (1950): 20, accessed January 7, 2015, doi: 10.1017/S003467050004571X.
[7] "World Government," Stanford Encyclopedia of Philosophy, accessed November 5, 2015, http://plato.stanford.edu/entries/world-government/.
[8] Hongying Wang, James N. Rosenau, "China and Global Governance," *Asian Perspective* 33 (2009): 5, accessed September 3, 2015, http://www.jstor.org/stable/42704681 and http://www.cebri.org/midia/documentos/05.pdf.
[9] Wm. Bross Lloyd Jr., "The United Nations and the World Federalism," *The Antioch Review* 9 (1949): 17, accessed February 10, 2015, http://www.jstor.org/stable/4609313.

(v) „All human beings are directly connected to a single centre of political power."[10]

4. There are some elements of today's nation state that the world state will mirror and use on a larger scale (make the transition from national to worldwide application and existence) soon after its establishment; the extended nature of the elements of the nation state are embodied in the conceptual, terminological and etymological nature of the 'world state':

(1) since there is only one state for the entire population of the planet:

(1.1) the world state will represent the population only inside the planet, not outside, because there is no other state with which the world state to interact;

(1.11) if the world state is going to represent the population of the Earth externally, then the representation is only possible to aliens who come to Earth, or the Earth (via the world state) is invited by aliens to represent the interest of its citizens (in politics, economics, culture, social, ecology etc.);

---

10 Ronald Tinnevelt, "Federal World Government," 221.

(I.III) the only natural border of the world state will be the atmosphere;

(II) the world state will be a mix of elements that represent the multiple identities (such as ethnicity, race, culture, language, etc.) of people;

(III) the components that make up the world state are the same as in today's national state, but there will be: one form of government (parliamentary and democratic republic), one economic system (free or mixed, obviously capitalism because the communist economic system proved catastrophic for the population), a single citizenship, a homogeneous social environment, many different cultures, religions and languages;

(IV) the world state will give rise to the formation of a common history, but not just any history, but the history of the first world state;

(V) there is a solution, probably disputed by a consistent majority, but which, for the sake of the coexistence of the humans, must be taken into account: giving up the ethnic and national name, i.e. the Romanian, Kurdish, Palestinian, Turkish, German, Brazilian, English, American and the rest; why? I have three answers:

24

(**v.i**) the ethnic and national name is subjective, formed over the years, it could be another name; it is not given by a divine power, by the creator; it was developed, proposed, accepted and spread by people;

(**v.ii**) because these names carry a history of conflicts between people; giving up and accepting a new name, for example 'earth citizen' - because we all live on planet Earth (and this name is subjective, but it is only one, not hundreds)-, 'cosmopolitan' (it will better represent the reality: we will be citizens of the whole planet, and since we don't know if there is life on other planets, we are the only citizens of the universe), it's a sacrifice that could bring a new history for humanity, it can offer a new era of the human being; a single identity, 'earth citizen' or 'cosmopolitan', for everyone, could make things much easier and help to eliminate the hatred that exists today between countries, nations, ethnic groups and so forth; currently, each country has a certain identity (behavior, traditions, culture) that is directly associated with the people living in that country; however, although this identity exists, it is not valid for all residents, but for a majority (most of the countries have their own minority which is a group with a different ethnicity than the majority, it can be by race,

25

language (different dialect), traditions etc.);
in the world state, the commission of an
inappropriate act will not be associated
with the entire population of the Earth; in
addition, the world state does not provide a
chance for another ethnic group to take
advantage of the inappropriate act to make
known a policy of hatred and rejection
towards the group to which the offender
belongs; in the world state, the way of life,
personality and behavior of a citizen will be
associated only with the person in question,
not with all human beings who belong to the
world state; giving up the ethnic and
national name makes it possible to create a
common global identity at the basic level:
we are all earth citizens or cosmopolitans,
but some bad, some good, schizophrenic,
frivolous, liars, passionate and so forth; a
single identity helps us to see the human
behind the name of an ethnic or national
group; everything we do will be between
earth citizens or cosmopolitans, that is,
humans, not between Romanians and Roma,
between Americans and Russians, between
Chinese and Japanese;

(v.III) dropping the race names: Caucasoid,
Negroid, Mongoloid; the major benefit is
that, in case of an illegality, the perpetrator
is presented without highlighting the colour
of the skin, and therefore does not put
pressure on the colour group to which it

26

belongs; the seriousness of the act and the methods of justice for the victim will be highlighted; such a decision can help to create a more homogeneous and united society; this solution is good if it is also applied in all existing forms (from birth certificate to employment forms), i.e. the box with the presentation of ethnicity and skin colour should no longer exist;

(VI) in this paper the concept 'world state' is used and replaces the term 'earth country', i.e. a single country.

5. Despite the changes brought about by the world state, many elements of today's countries will be preserved. Here are some of them:

(I) the world state will be recognized exactly as it happens in the case of the current national state: by the population of the country, that is, by the entire population of the Earth;

(II) the world state will do its duty exactly as it happens in today's countries: based on the rights and obligations written in the system of laws and the constitution voted by the population;

(III) in today's countries a supreme political authority will be preserved, it will be a

27

governor as it is in the states of the United States of America (USA);

(ıv) in the world state, the population of today's countries will still live in their country, they will not be displaced;

(v) the public administration will continue to exist; the institutions of the former country will continue to represent and take care of the population, but will be subordinated to the central authority at the level of the Earth, i.e. the world state; for example, Romania's entry into the European Union (EU): Romania has preserved and even strengthened its state institutions and obeys the European legislation voted in Brussels, the capital of the EU;

(vı) a capital at the level of the Earth, where the headquarters of the world state would be, then one in each continent and at the level of today's countries (may remain Bucharest, Warsaw, Berlin, Budapest, etc.);

(vıı) the principle of local autonomy will be preserved.

6. Often, in specialized literature, there are several reunions of terms used in a single formula and usage to express the same meaning. It is also the case of the world state. We have the following relationship of

28

equality of different terms, but which, for me at least, refer to the same meaning: one authority for all the population of the Earth. Here is the equality of the terms:

> world state = global state = world government = global government.

II. What is 'Goal'?

1. 'Goal' means "aim, purpose, scope, end, result, final achievement."[11] Of course, we are not talking about the right or wrong way to achieve the goal, but we are only talking about the result or the end that we want to achieve, to reach. A goal can be to buy a new pair of shoes, run two kilometers, get the highest grade, get married, etc.

2. The concept of 'goal' is as misleading as many other concepts. Why? Because, as Frederick Dunn notes, "it suggests that what we want has clear limits."[12] The goal may be precise, that is, we know that we want to become mayor of a city, but the path to the

---

[11] In this paper I define and use 'goal' as 'scope' from Frederick S. Dunn, "The Scope of International Relations," *World Politics* 1 (1948): 142, accessed December 22, 2012, doi: 10.2307/2009164; "Scop," Dexonline.ro, accessed October 21, 2015, https://dexonline.ro/definitie/scop; "Scope," Dictionary.reference.com, accessed October 21, 2015, http://dictionary.reference.com/browse/scope; "Goal," Dictionary.reference.com, accessed October 21, 2015, http://dictionary.reference.com/browse/goal.
[12] Frederick S. Dunn, "The Scope," 142.

result is not a fixed one but, as Dunn writes, "is constantly changing,"[13] and, precisely because of this, there is a chance that the goal will not be reached. We want to buy a pair of shoes, but we can't find the size we need, the color we like, or the quality is poor for a price higher than our available budget. However, there is the situation where sometimes we can achieve the *total goal* (got the desired grade) and sometimes we can achieve a *part of the goal* (because of a wild animal, we ran only one kilometer).

3. The nature of the goal is misleading because the primary goal may be a positive action for the entity who created the goal, but it could be a negative end for another entity. Although we aim to achieve a positive goal, the final and unforeseen result can be a negative one. We buy the pair of shoes we love and fit in the budget, but after two weeks the shoes deteriorate faster than we expected and we have to spend more money than we previously planned; here the seller collected profit and fulfilled the purpose of the company, but we didn't get to enjoy the purchased product for a long term. A religious leader wants to build a community of believers who obey the customs of the religion it belongs to in order to create a harmonious world, but not all

---

[13] *Ibidem*, 142.

the people who were born into the same
religion group agree to keep hundreds of
years of old laws, where children with an
identity different from their own are not
accepted as part of the community (for
example, sexual attraction towards the
same sex, or the decision to abandon the
religion of which it is a part and embrace an
agnostic lifestyle); the religious leader
vehemently rejects any deviation from
customs and promotes a harsh approach of
the religion through acts of violence against
believers who challenge the promoted
status-quo; despite the desire to create a
harmonious world, from the point of view of
religious customs, the thinking of believers
in the same religious group has advanced
and they no longer believe in traditions, but
are willing to accept the biological and
psychological reality of their children, even
if it means creating of a fissure between the
medieval approach of their leader and the
objective and cosmopolitan reality in their
family.

4. It should be noted about the goals of the
world state that:

(1) some are already found in various
countries, for example some in Western
countries or between the USA states and the
EU countries;

WHAT IS 'goal'?

(II) are truly fulfilled only in the world state;

(III) some can only be obtained in the world state, such as the elimination of wars and the end of the struggle for power;

(IV) the extended and final nature of the goals can be obtained only after we have a world state;

(V) are a part of the total positive goals;

(VI) are a base from which to start the construction of the world state;

(VII) some goals can be achieved in second two after we have the world state, for example the elimination of international wars, other goals in months, years and decades, for example civilizational orientation;

(VIII) are interconnected and interdependent;

(IX) some goals are achieved only if we achieve other goals, for example eliminating world wars helps to achieve world peace; in other words, some goals are a side effect of achieving other goals;

33

(**x**) some countries can achieve the positive goals of the world state inside the country only by accepting and recognizing a world state, for example countries in Latin America, Europe, Asia and Africa;

(**xı**) On the origin of the goals of the world state:

ᴀ. goals directly associated with the world state: **ıı, xı, xıı, xııı, xıx, xv, xvı, xıx, xx, xxııı, xxv, xxvı, xxvıı, xxvııı, xxıx, xxx, xxxı, xxxıv, xxxvıı, xxxıx, xlvıı , xlvııı**.

ʙ. goals modified and presented as goals of the world state (here the authors have or have not made a weak association with the world state; I have transformed the weak or no association into a goal of the world state, I have considered that it can be a goal of the world state): **ı, ıı, ıv, vıı, xıı, xx, xxı, xxıı, xxx, xxxıı, xxxııı, xxxv, xxxvı, xxxıx, xl, xlv, xlvı, l**.

c. goals resulting from the mental exercise: **ı, ıı, ıı, ıv, v, vı, vııı, ıx, x, xıı, xııı, xıv, xvı, xvıı, xvııı, xıx, xxxı, xxıv, xxvıı, xxvııı, xxıx , xxx, xxxvııı, xlıı, xlııı, xlıv, xlv, xlvı, xlıx**.

(**xıı**) the title of the paper could also be according to the following combinations of terms:

WHAT IS 'goal'?

The Goals Of World State:
= Of The Global State
= Of The World Government
= Of The Global Government

or

*Problems That Can Be Solved In The World
State*:
= By The Global State
= By The World Government
= By The Global Government.

III. THE GOALS OF WORLD STATE

1. At general level, incorporated into a single theoretical body, there are eight positive goals of the world state:

(1) resolves for the first time and forever the following issues: **(1.1)** the war; **(1.11)** weapons of mass destruction - it will no longer be possible to threaten with biological, chemical and nuclear bombs, but could be maintained to be used against a possible enemy from outside the planet such as a meteorite, or maybe even other species-, and the arms market in general; **(1.111)** efficient distribution of natural resources; **(1.1V)** eliminating terrorism; **(1.V)** end of famine; **(1.VI)** reducing and then eliminating poverty; **(1.VII)** effective justice; **(1.VIII)** protecting and promoting human rights.

Why can these problems be solved only in the world state? I have two answers.

THE GOALS *OF* WORLD STATE

A. Due to existence of several forms of government, political ideologies and religious cults: monarchy, republic, theocracy, democracy, communism, Christianity, Islam, Hinduism etc. Every form of government and ideology has a set of ideas that decide how society should look like; currently, this set of ideas only favours its own population, and, specifically, protects a majority found in the set of ideas; a minority of the population from the same group that does not find/identify with the set of ideas are considered enemies, which creates a conflict of vision of human life with its own citizens, which, unfortunately, sometimes develops into a civil war and negative personal relations for long term (decades and centuries). Because the set of ideas is a representation of the majority, the minority remains exposed and often becomes the target of physical aggression, possibly direct or indirect extinction, suffers the consequences of the existence of laws that reduce their presence from the total life of the society; this plurality of sets of ideas makes it difficult to achieve the above goals inside the nation state and between countries.

B. Because the world state includes the entire population of the Earth and, as a result, we will all be citizens of the same state and country, and have the same rights

37

and obligations. It will be a common society, so we will have the same norms and values, even if we are living in Africa, the North Pole, on an island in the Pacific Ocean or in Canada. Being one state and one country, the state will be obliged to ensure the well-being of all people on Earth. In addition, some current countries can solve the above problems only by their political integration into a larger state unit. Since we will be citizens of the same state, today's rich and powerfull countries, such as the USA, Great Britain, Germany, France, China, Russia, Japan, will be legally, morally and spiritually obliged to export companies, technology and know-how (specific knowledge) to help current economically underdeveloped countries to develop without signing treaties and agreements with positive effects only for one party: that is, to have jobs, to afford the economic product, thus managing to reduce and, over time, to eliminate hunger and poverty.

(II) To select the best methods, theories and laws for humans, fauna and flora; the best form of government (many theorists agree with the parliamentary republic) political ideology (democracy), economic system (capitalism), social system etc.

(III) Export and expansion of methods, theories and laws from those countries that

are well-functioning in all other countries
on Earth that does not work well, thus
making a functional world system.

(IV) Achieving at world level and in all
current countries the five social values to
which all states support and want, but
cannot be achieved individually: security,
freedom, order, justice and welfare.[14] A
world state is more likely for these social
values to be achieved in all current
countries, also in those countries where
they do not exist or exist but are weakly
developed. Why? The answer that I wrote
above is also valid here: because the world
state will comprise the entire Earth's
population and, as a result, we will all be
citizens of the same state and country. We
will all have the same rights and obligations.
It cannot make the slightest difference, even
if we live in the North Pole or in the middle
of the Pacific Ocean.

(v) The goals written by Nicholas Hagger in
his book *The World Government: A Blueprint
for a Universal World State*:

„**(v.1)** bringing peace between nation-state
and disarmament;

---

[14] Robert H. Jackson, Georg Sørensen, *Introduction to
International Relations: Theories and Approaches*, Fifth
Edition (London, New York: Oxford University Press, 2013):
5.

(v.ii) sharing natural resources and energy so that all humankind can have a raised standard of living;

(v.iii) solving environmental problems such a global warming, which seem to be beyond self-interested nation-states;

(v.iv) where possible, ending disease;

(v.v) where possible, ending famine;

(v.vi) solving the world's financial crisis;

(v.vii) where possible, redistributing wealth to eliminate poverty."[15]

(vi) The goals of the *Charter of the United Nations* signed 26 June 1945, modified, adjusted to world state, valid and respected much better that today in all current countries:

(vi.i) to maintain international peace and security: to take effective collective measures for the prevention and removal of threats to the peace, and for the suppression of acts of aggression or other

---

[15] Nicholas Hagger, *The World Government: A Blueprint for a Universal World State* (Washington: O-Books, 2010): 73-74.

breaches of the peace, and to bring about by peaceful means, and in conformity with the principles of justice and the system of laws, adjustment or settlement of disputes or situations which might lead to a breach of the peace;

(VI.II) to develop friendly relations among humans based on respect for the principle of equal rights and self-determination of peoples, and to take other appropriate measures to strengthen universal peace;

(VI.III) to achieve international co-operation in solving world problems of an economic, social, cultural, or humanitarian character, and in promoting and encouraging respect for human rights and for fundamental freedoms for all without distinction as to race, sex, language, culture or religion;

(VI.IV) to be a centre for harmonising the actions of humans in the attainment of these common ends.[16]

(VII) The EU objectives changed and adapted to a world state:

---

[16] See "Charter of the United Nations," United Nations, last accessed December 3, 2015, http://www.un.org/en/charter-united-nations/.

(VII.I) promoting economic and social progress, the ultimate goal being the realisation of the single market and the single currency;

(VII.II) affirming human identity by a common security and defence policy;

(VII.III) establish *global citizenship*: offers the same rights and obligations to all citizens of the Earth;

(VII.IV) to develop an area of freedom, security and justice, by co-operation in justice and internal affairs;

(VII.V) to develop and to respect the acquis of the world state.

Additionally, we have the **(VII.VI)** four freedoms *(VII.VI.I)* freedom of travel *(VII.I.II)* work. *(VII.VI.III)* services and *(VII.VI.IV)* capital.[17]

(VIII) *The Universal Declaration of Human Rights* applied to legitimate and the only law

---

[17] European Union, *Aims and Values*, available at: https://european-union.europa.eu/principles-countries-history/principles-and-values/aims-and-values_en, last accessed: October 24, 2022.

for human rights on Earth and current countries.[18]

2. In this paper I explored fifty positive goals of the world state, which is sufficient to construct a balance of the goals of the world state. Before I start the extended description of the goals, I must make a few clarifications about their sources of existence and necessity:

(I) are the wishes of philosophers, political scientists, sociologists, lawyers, poets and all the ordinary humans of Earth, from past to present and future, who are in search for a better lifestyle;

(II) are what humanity needs to live in peace and prosperity;

(III) exists in the domestic and foreign policy strategy of the countries, but cannot be achieved individually in the complete form;

---

[18] See "The Universal Declaration of Human Rights," United Nations, last accessed December 3, 2015, http://www.un.org/en/universal-declaration-human-rights/. An author associated this goal with world state, but I don't remember the title of the paper, nor there is any written notes about it.

(IV) exists in international governmental and non-governmental organisations strategies that promotes a better world;

(V) the goals are found in all areas of human activity;

(VI) some goals are associated only with the world state (elimination of wars), others are an extension of them, but it is precisely this extension that makes them function at their maximum capacity (global democracy, world free market);

(VII) some goals are reproduced as I found them, others modified and proposed;

(VIII) the authors used in this research paper *should not be seen as the only source* of the positive goals of the world state: *I have used a small part* of the existing scientific sources.

3. For each positive goal, I have tried to show examples that: (I) provide a more adequate understanding of the problems that exist today and can have a better end in the world state; (II) can move the human imagination regarding the process of action of the positive goals; (III) the examples are limited and, for this reason, I invite each reader to reflect on them, for example whether the existence of a world state can

44

really help to create a stronger world community prepared to truly fight for the future of all identities, or to intervene with positive examples to contribute to the narrative of the construction and research of the world state.

4. The positive goals of the world state are:

(1). TO ACCEPT, TO BUILD AND TO SIGN A WORLD OR GLOBAL SOCIAL CONTRACT. [19]

It means the extension of the social contract from national to world or global level. All

---

[19] Jean-Jacques Rousseau, *The Social Contract Or Principles of Political Right,* (1762), accessed July 4, 2015, https://www.marxists.org/reference/subject/economics/rousseau/social-contract/index.htm, electronic edition; Martha C. Nussbaum, "Beyond the Social Contract: Toward Global Justice," *The Tanner Lectures on Human Values*, (Australian National University, Canberra November 12 and 13, 2002 and at Clare Hall, University of Cambridge, March 5 and 6, 2003): 415-507, accessed September 24, 2015, http://tannerlectures.utah.edu/_documents/a-to-z/n/nussbaum_2003.pdf; Martha C. Nussbaum, "Beyond the Social Contract: Capabilities and Global Justice," *Oxford Development Studies* 32 (2004): 3-18, accessed September 25, 2015, doi: 10.1080/1360081042000184093; Jason Neidleman, 9 octombrie 2012, "The Social Contract Theory in a Global Context," *E-International Relations*, accessed October 4, 2015, http://www.e-ir.info/2012/10/09/the-social-contract-theory-in-a-global-context/; Jeff Faux, "Toward a Global Social Contract," *Economic Policy Institute*, accessed October 4, 2015, http://www.epi.org/publication/webfeatures_viewpoints_mexico_grand_bargain/.

Earth's population will create the first and the last voluntary civil agreement between them whereby each individual will become a member of the first human world community, then the first world state. Instead, the individual will receive the same rights and obligations as the community.

(II). TO BECOME CITIZENS OF PLANET EARTH.[20]

---

[20] Fariborz Moshirian, "The Significance of a World Government in the Process of Globalisation in the 21st Century," *Journal of Banking & Finance* 32 (2008): 1434, accessed September 5, 2015, doi:10.1016/j.jbankfin.2008.03.004. It is known as (i) cosmopolitanism: derives from the Greek word *kosmopolitês* and means citizen of the world; universal citizenship; an ideology that says that all people belong to a single community, based on a sharing moral laws; free of local, provincial and national ideas, the house is all the world; see the following sources: "Cosmopolitism," Dex.ro, accessed October 21, 2015, http://www.dex.ro/cosmopolitism; "Cosmopolitanism," Dictionary.reference.com, accessed October 23, 2015, http://dictionary.reference.com/browse/cosmopolitanism; "Cosmopolitanism," Stanford Encyclopedia of Philosophy, accessed October 23, 2015, http://plato.stanford.edu/entries/cosmopolitanism/; Gustavo Lins Ribeiro, *What is Cosmopolitanism?*, accessed October 23, 2015, http://www.vibrant.org.br/downloads/v2n1_wc.pdf; (ii) global citizen: it's a person who identifies not only national but global, i.e. with people from other countries and actions that helps to develop the world, such as poverty reduction, care for environmental, saving species of animals and plants; identifies as a member of the whole human

We are currently citizens of a country that owns a part of the Earth's territory. It is separated by natural borders (oceans, rivers, mountains, forests, lakes) and artificial borders (checkpoints, border zones, demilitarised zones). Neighbouring populations have no right to everything that exists in a country, but the population is allowed to transit the country as tourists (for a short period of time: hours or a few days, depending on the means of transport; on the basis of a passport and a visa, for a limited period of time: a few days or months, usually three months); few people can move permanently (provided that certain eligibility conditions are met according with the laws of the country to which one is moving, but different, more or less, by the country of their origins); to maintain and create a business with different companies (at the base is a commercial treaty signed between at least two countries).

In the world state, each individual becomes a citizen of planet Earth. The *foreigner* disappears from the country, but

community on Earth. See: Elizabeth Kruempelmann, *The Global Citizen: a Guide to Creating an International Life and Career* (Berkeley: Ten Speed Press, 2002); William E. Scheuerman, "Cosmopolitanism and the World State," *Review of International Studies* 40 (2014), accessed April 14, 2014, doi: 10.1017/S0260210513000417.

the stranger/newcomer will exist, in the sense that we do not know the personality and character of the humans until the moment we come into contact. This citizenship begins with the individual freedom of thinking, religion and expression. Global and singular citizenship will give the right to a family, to a job, to travel and access to a property anywhere in the world.

An advanced and efficient housing system can be better guaranteed by the world state: access to accomodation free of charge and according to own's need, and for life without the right of eviction by the world state for any reason against the tenant; moreover, the new housing system should not follow the current system because the price changes according to the economic system, where there is a greater chance of paying hugely for a house that does not reflect the price in reality, and puts unnecessary pressure on citizens; furthermore, some current landlords raise the price to increase their profit from year to year, and a hostile relationship develops between citizens; in the end, after death, the only way is to God, and houses, physical objects, will remain on Earth.

The elimination of the struggle for a property, and the assurance from the world government that it is willing to provide free housing without rent and tax, is a generous

48

and welcome development for citizens that will enormously strengthen the support for the idea of world union towards a more just and secure world; at the same time, free housing can be provided only if the citizens in need provide evidence with a secure job and are willing to contribute to the welfare of the society.

Of course, one can retain the right to a property even if the world government is going to be the institution that built the house for free, for example to fulfill the right to privacy and family.

In the world state, moving will be much more efficient and faster: either citizens accept the free housing offered by the world government, or can buy a house created by a famous architect, or build the house according to own's vision (we can keep this idea, in the sense that the housing system provided by the world government should be made to meet basic needs and fixed models, but at the same time we can celebrate human creativity by granting the right to buy land and build a house according with your own vision, aspirations and budget).

The movement of citizens to a territory other than the one in which they were born will be done as simply as moving inside current countries, for example: a citizen from Sibiu (Romania) can live or buy a house in Beijing (China) as simple and fast as one can rent or buy a house in Iasi (Romania): without living in Iasi, without having been born in Iasi, without being part of the same ethnic group and region.

There will no longer be a transit of a foreign country, but an internal transit of the same country. To visit a different territory (or former national country) we no longer need to obtain a tourist visa. As for the definitive move, it will be possible as if it were a movement within inside the current nation states, but, due to linguistic difference and barriers, we will have to know or have a digital device to help us to understand the language spoken in the territory where we move, otherwise we may encounter difficulties in building a more friendly relationship.

North Koreans can see their relatives in South Korea again. Israelis will be able to go quietly in the Palestinian National Authority and vice versa. No one can take them out anymore. Palestinians will be able to go to another country and return back to Israel and the Palestinian National Authority. There is only one world state, one country and one citizenship. Each territory (present countries) will become the home of all the people on Earth who want to live in that territory. No one will be kicked out of the country again.

We can candidate anywhere on the planet for a public position of mayor, councilor or member of parliament as is happening today in the USA and the EU. However, for effective communication, we must know the language of the village, city or country where we want to candidate. Moreover, in order to fulfill the role of the position at the expected level, it is good to have the following requirement: the citizens who want to candidate for a more important position, must provide evidence of residence of at least 5 years in the specific community + evidence of involvement in activities in different sectors of the community; even better if the candidate is able to prove a rich experience in a specific field of activity, which can enrich the results and the experience of the community.

Natural borders will continue to exist, and will separate territories with ethnic groups, but this separation will only exist until the day when, in each current territory, a homogeneous group with multiple identities of race, ethnicity, and language is formed.

(III). A SINGLE CONSTITUTION.

It means that all people from Earth will have the same rights and obligations. It will replace the current country's constitution and will be available in all current countries. The existence of one global social contract

51

strengthens the moral and spiritual ties between people of Earth.

(IV). ONE FORM OF GOVERNMENT.[21]

The most acceptable form of government for the entire population of the Earth is the parliamentary republic, obviously democratic. The other forms of government will disappear forever: monarchy, directorial system (Switzerland), communism, theocracy (Iran, Vatican) and so on. The pluralism of political parties will be preserved (social democrats, liberals, greens, conservatives and so on). As for the representation of the population in the world government, the procedure will be the same as in the case of EU members of parliament: each territory will choose its representatives by free and direct vote. It will be a global democratic gain.

(V). A SINGLE SYSTEM OF LAWS IN ALL THE FIELDS OF HUMAN ACTIVITY:

from economic, social (including health and education), political, ecological, cultural, legal, to religious ones.

A single system of laws for the entire population of the Earth, as it happens in

---

[21] Hans J. Morgenthau, *Politica între naţiuni,* 523.

today's countries, will make things simpler and easier to achieve. For example, the penalties for breaking criminal laws differ greatly between countries. It happens that for the same crime (being in a homosexual relationship) in one country the sanction is capital punishment by execution or prison time, while in another country you are free to make your own choices.

The world state provides a single system of punishment for all law-breaking citizens; if we're going to steal a chicken or a phone in California, most likely it won't be necessary, but hypothetically speaking, the punishment will be the same as in Argentina, Burkina Faso or Finland.

Also, a single system of laws will eliminate, for example, the extradition law. Today if an American citizen steals fifty million dollars from a pension system, in a few hours the citizen can end up in China. Once in China, the citizen cannot be extradited. The damage remains, the future retirees without a pension, and the thief will live in wealth until runs out of money or dies. If an American or Russian commits a voluntary or involuntary crime in Romania, the American or Russian is extradited and tried under American and Russian law, and vice versa. The same thing happens in Romania: whoever breaks the laws and wants to escape punishment, can take refuge in Israel, and vice versa, there is no extradition treaty between Romania and Israel. In the world state, the American, Romanian, Israeli or Russian can be tried anywhere in the world without any intervention from the authorities in the territory where the citizen was born or is resident: the laws and the legal system existing in the USA and Russia are also applied in Romania and Israel.

In the case of religion, the most controversial and sensitive topic of the world state, and for the sake of human coexistence, religious indoctrination in all schools on Earth can be prohibited by world law. For a better lifestyle, the divine laws, which are applied in certain countries in the form of legal laws, can be replaced by legal laws based on the real ontology of the people. Why? Because divine laws, or considered divine, being against some human identities (for example against homosexuals, atheists, agnostics) do not correspond to objective human reality, it violates the rights to freedom of expression, and physical security. Homosexuals, atheists and agnostics are physically assaulted and even sentenced to death for what they are, and because they refuse to obey the laws written in books considered divine.

In the world state, being a unique law in the economic field, the countries considered today as tax havens will disappear. All people will register the income to pay taxes

54

and fees, because only in this way will we have a functioning financial world system.

In the world state, at least theoretically, no one can hide from the legal system. However, even if it is the world state, people will try to cheat the laws exactly as it happens today. This fact should not scare us, humans are not robots to follow instruction everytime. There will always be people who don't want to obey the law, who think they are above the law, and others who will break it by mistake.

Finally, for a better efficiency of the world state, the principle of local autonomy will be preserved.

(VI). ALL HUMAN BEINGS CONNECTED TO THE SAME SYSTEM OF VALUES

such as individual freedom, free choices, equality, peace, openness to change, tolerance, affection, empathy, respect, etc.

(VII). THE RECOGNITION OF ALL IDENTITIES[22]: from racial (Negroid,

---

[22] The struggle for recognition see Alexander Wendt, "Why a World State," 507-514; 'thin' recognition (being acknowledge as an independent subject within a community of law) and 'thick' recognition (being respected for what makes a person special or unique) see Alexander Wendt, "Why a World State," 511-512. Also see Lisa Strömbom, "Thick Recognition: Advancing Theory on

Caucasoid and Mongoloid), national (Brazilian, German, Hungarian, Argentinian and so on), religious (Christian, Buddhist, Hindu, atheist and so on), of those people considered without a country (for example Kurds and Roma -in the countries where they live are considered ethnic minorities-) to ethnic minorities who have their own country, but have emigrated to another country, up to the one offered by the sexual orientation (heterosexual or one of the sexual orientations included in LGBT+).

(VIII). NO IDENTITY WILL BE SACRIFICED TO FULFILL THE WISHES OF OTHER IDENTITY.

Currently, political and religious leaders, in order to win as many believers and sympathizers as possible to literally obey the divine laws, are willing to sacrifice people with preferences, habits and sexual orientation different from that of the majority and, moreover, their own. For example, rockers, because they have a more pronounced musical preference, are labeled by religious leaders as Satanists, and that whoever listens to such music will end up in hell. Some political and religious leaders,

Identity Change in Intractable Conflicts," *European Journal of International Relations* 20 (2014): 168-191, accessed August 12, 2015, doi: 10.1177/1354066112439217.

and the wider mass of believers (ultra and radicals) are confident that homosexuals were sent by God to test their faith in divinity. Rejecting homosexuals, sometimes through physical aggression and murder, is accepted by believers as a good solution to please the deity they worship, believing that they will thus escape divine and final punishment. In fact, labeling some people as Satanists and rejecting them through physical aggression and murder, it violates the human right to freedom of choice, expression, image and life; believers, political and religious leaders become a threat factor to the physical and individual security of rockers, which creates a visible contradiction between the moral values existing in the customs of religion (such as the idea of a harmonious world and created in the vision of God), and the practice performed by neighbors and family members. Homosexuals did not choose to be born homosexual, they simply are homosexual; they have dreams, feelings, desires like the heterosexual man. Sacrificing the life of a person with a different identity is the same as sacrificing the life of a heterosexual. Why should homosexuals give up their lives for the happiness of religious leaders and believers? It should be the other way around: political, religious leaders and believers to put some effort and get the

57

courage to question the existence of a God and the books considered divine; furthermore, to accept the human reality, which is given through the lens of biology and anthropology.

(IX). TO SAVE SPECIES OF ANIMALS AND PLANTS.

All animals and plants on Earth become the interest of all people on Earth. The animals and plants of Africa will be of interest to the people of the USA. Why? Because animals and plants in Africa are part of the same country, even if they are thousands of kilometres away from the USA.

Currently there are groups of people who, for profit, are willing to exterminate animals and plant species. A unique legislation on the planet, and the only one existing in all territories, whose existence and application is offered and protected by the world state, makes possible the definitive elimination at the level of the Earth of the extermination of animals and the disappearance of plants. Of course, in order to achieve this goal, a unique law and the necessary technology must be invented to reduce pollution, because pollution is also an effect of the disappearance of plants and animals.

(X). EDUCATION FOR ALL.

One of the positive effects of education is
the elimination of the cult of personality
(pupils and students will no longer be
forced to revere, even deify, their leader, as
is happening today in North Korea and
other countries) and the religious
indoctrination of future generations.

Through education, the system of
religious ideas promoted today through
fear, false and negative end of people who
refuse to accept it, will be eliminated
forevermore. Through education one will
learn and find out two truths: (i) all people
are equal regardless of race, culture,
language, religion, sexual orientation; (ii)
those who are different, but demonized
today by certain groups, are wrong in life, if
not less, as those who accuse them of
blasphemy and sins.

The entire population will have the
same educational system; people will be
able to learn in any school on Earth, like in
today's countries. Women's and children's
rights are marginalized and locked up in an
oppressive and unjust patriarchal system.
Women, through the same education as
men, can develop intellectually and
intervene with solutions to overcome
humanitarian crises. As far as children are

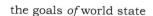

concerned, a universal law can be created to prohibits any kind of physical and mental abuse that can be sanctioned at the same level anywhere in the world. Children need to develop their intellectual capacity to be able to understand the world they live in and the problems they will face later; children should not be forced to work illegally in squalid conditions and paid less for the work performed, but should be protected and raised in dignity and respect because, in the end, they will become adults and have to decide the development of the next stages of the world state for them and for the next generations.

(XI). HEALTH FOR ALL.

Since there will be only one state, the state has the moral and legal obligation to ensure access to medical services in all current countries and at the same advanced level everywhere.

Access to the healthcare system will be a right as important as the right to free speech, and it will be available in every hospital on the planet. As a safety measure that the population does not take advantage of the medical system, a condition can be imposed: access to the health system is free for any illness only if the citizen provide evidence of having a job, or is unable to work due to health reasons (the better lifestyle available in the world state, should decrease the number of patients and difficult-to-treat diseases).

(XII). JUSTICE.[23]

Currently, due to national sovereignty, countries reserve the right to do justice, which, sometimes, is outside the democratic norms; today there is a tradition that justice is bought and the perpetrator becomes the victim and the victim becomes the perpetrator; in serious cases, kidnapping, death threats, political blackmail, and even war are resorted to. Being one state, there will be one legal system for everyone. Today's countries will no longer be able to do justice according to their own historically inherited conceptions. All disagreements between territories will be resolved only in a court, without weapons. The punishment for breaking some laws will not be the total destruction of the one who loses or control over natural resources,

---

[23] Stefan Gosepath, "The Global Scope of Justice," *Metaphilosophy* 32 (2001):153, accessed September 5, 2015, doi: 10.1111/1467-9973.00179; Luis Cabrera, "Global Government and the Sources of Globoscepticism," *Millenium: Journal of International Studies* 43 (2015): 476, accessed January 28, 2015, doi: 10.1177/0305829814541833.

plus a negative management of the population, but stiff fines or imprisonment.

At the individual level, in the world state, there will be a greater chance than at present for a fair trial, especially for those citizens who today live in countries with a legal system formed according to religious and mediaeval norms. Adequate education and the fulfilment of basic needs will reduce, maybe even completely eliminate corruption from the legal system.

(XIII). FREEDOM OF EXPRESSION.

Currently, there are many countries that have as their basis the reduction and even prohibition of freedom of speech, more specifically, prohibits the promotion of a discourse that challenges the narrative line of the government, or of companies and organisations that want to promote a narrative line for their own benefit.

In the last four years the population of the Western world has been subjected to a system of 'cancel culture' in which citizens (most of the time famous and rich people) who challenged the methods of discussions about certain social movements online and in the public space, were 1. penalised by companies that own social media applications and other valuable and popular products; 2. pseudonymous users sent

62

death threats to users who challenged the narrative line promoted online and in the public space. This penalty was issued because the narrative of various social movements was challenged with evidence that show the weakness of the arguments launched. More often than this, the citizens who challenged the narrative of a social movement, the penalty resulted in articles written and published by Western mass-media that portray the individual's opinion as dangerous for other people, although the social movement that promoted a particular opinion demanded the right to express that opinion without restriction; in other words, there is a visible contradiction and an injustice for all the parties involved.

In the world state, a system like 'cancel culture' will not exist because it will offer the same rights to everyone, even if the opinion expressed does not follow the narrative line expected by a specific group. Disagreeing with the opinion of others is a right that no one can take away, and social media companies will not have the power to decide the limits of human rights and decide per se and arbitrarily who is right and who is wrong. Obviously, there is a difference between expressing an opinion using appropriate language and showing tolerance towards the individual or group about whom the opinion is expressed, and the opinion expressed inversely proportional to the example above, and delivered through acts of physical violence and threats made online and in the public space with the aim of discouraging such opinion; in this case, social media companies must intervene, because the safety of users must be taken into account, and the space made available, mostly free, must be verified, so that each person and identity can be protected from possible abuse (verbal and written) and represented in a civilised manner.

(XIV). FREEDOM OF RELIGION.

Today there are many countries that refuse to accept other religions. Such a restriction is especially supported by religious groups who believe that the religion they promote is true; moreover, religious freedom is prohibited because the set of ideas at the base is weak and the argument for validating its existence, as a good product for society, can be comfortably combated; the granting of religious freedom, meaning the existence and acceptance of multiple religions within the same nation-state, leads to the creation of public pressure against those who control the set of religious ideas; the major consequence of religious freedom against the set of religious ideas can lead to the collapse of an entire society, it can

64

create a civil war (like India with Pakistan) which can last for decades. As a world state, freely chosen by the entire population of the planet, the set of religious ideas will no longer be generated by a religious group that has placed itself above all and decides which religion is better, truer and wiser for people; the citizens who have the opportunity and understand the consequences of religious freedom, will choose to express freely their desire to follow the religion they consider good for private life without interfering negatively in the lives of other groups, because the world state has at its disposal the necessary measures to stop this attitude between citizens of the same state.

One God for the entire population of the planet is probably the best solution, since biologically and spiritually we all have the same structure and, therefore, the logical answer is that we all have the same creator.

The God described in some books considered divine does not offer an equal and positive end for women, but, strangely enough, keeps roughly the same system of rewards already existing in the physical world: after the transition to the eternal, men will be rewarded better in comparison to women. There is even a visible global culture of viewing women as less useful than men, which is wrong.

A new world system can reset the religious system and promote a divine end for women equal to that of men, and where God ends up offering the same punishment or reward regardless of biological sex, a system where the soul and actions performed in the physical reality to represent in truth the reward and the sanction received after death.

Since *we do not know for sure that there is a God*, the world state can provide a new and advanced God from the current version; the world state can leave behind the God of vengeance and eternal punishment for a sin committed for a few minutes (the sin can be committed out of love and care in order to provide a sense of protection and security that cannot be guaranteed under other conditions according to human thinking at the time of committing the sin); the world state can present a God who offers love and understanding just as parents do it (or should do it) with their children: regardless of sex, colour and sexual orientation.

(XV). FREEDOM OF THINKING.

This goal retains the essence written in goals *(XIII). FREEDOM OF EXPRESSION* and *(XIV). RELIGIOUS FREEDOM*. One of the biggest changes brought about by the world state is the reflection of private thinking (carried inside the mind of each citizen) into the public space exactly as it exists and has been formed, and this right will offer the most compared to today's nation state: let's stop lying to each other! We constantly live in a state of fear that our opinions will hurt us back, and at the same time we see that we are right, and we cannot say it because we do not have enough trust in the state institutions and the people voted by us to protect our way of thinking, lifestyle and based on the choices we made.

(XVI). TO OPEN THE BORDERS, FREE MOVEMENT ACROSS THE PLANET AT ANY TIME.[24]

I estimate that between 90-95% of the planet's population have not travelled to another country. Probably 50% of the population of the planet has not travelled outside the county they belong to, and probably 30-40% have not left the village where they were born and live. One reason is the current economic system: many countries are poorly developed and citizens cannot afford to travel; there is a lack of a transport system with functional and available streets and highways in villages and cities; another reason is the legislative

---

[24] Ronald Tinnevelt, "Federal World Government," 231.

system of the states: to travel to another state we need an invitation from a citizen or sometimes from a hotel, then a visa issued by the administrative system of the country where we want to travel. Finally, a trip becomes expensive; there are many papers to pay and many roads to walk to get the right paperwork. Another cause is the political system. For example, Uzbekistan, Eritrea and Somalia are not very open to tourists. North Korea has an extrem tourist system: if we manage to get a visa, we can only visit the country if we have a North Korean companion with us; any travel outside the capital is possible only with the approval of the authorities.[25] One final cause is internal conflicts and most of them are in the countries of Africa, the Middle East, South America and West Asia; in these parts of the world, criminal groups resort to kidnapping tourists in order to demand a reward in exchange for their release.

In the world state, the natural borders between today's countries will be considered internal borders of the state; the Western Alps, the natural border between Switzerland and Italy, so different states and citizens, will be seen as the Southern Carpathians in Romania: a natural border between counties of Hunedoara, Alba, Sibiu

---

[25] "Coreea de Nord," Guvernul României, Ministerul Afacerilor Externe, accessed November 23, 2015, http://www.mae.ro/travel-conditions/3685.

and Braşov and the counties of Gorj, Vâlcea and Dâmboviţa. Although artificial borders will be eliminated, especially those borders made of fences, there still need to be checkpoints in certain locations to check the compliance of citizens with the law, as is happening today in the EU.

A positive effect is travelling to all places on Earth without a passport and without a visa, as it happens today in the USA and the EU: just with identity card. Moreover, in order to provide superior services in comparision with the current nation state, the world state will have the power to provide access to the air transport system without the control of an identity card and based only on a valid travel ticket. Furthermore, thanks to the advanced technology that is available today and highly more advanced tomorrow, citizens' data can be secured in a simple QR code that can be scanned anywhere to prove our identity to the world state without third parties (transport companies, payments in shops, courier companies, etc.); a simple sentence on the screen of a device (for example *Correct information* in green colour) to be enough to guarantee the existence of a real identity and confirmed by the computer system of the world state. In this way, in a few hours we will be able to admire the sunset from Paris or Jakarta, we can take pictures while crossing the natural

69

border with a train from the region of Turkey to Syria, we can travel by boat to Somalia without encountering traffickers at sea, mobsters and pirates, all done without our details being shared across multiple computer systems that could be subject to a possible cyber attack (being a world state, cyber attacks between citizens of different states will be eliminated, and remains only the own government as enemy, which is the world state itself), or the information system may be inactive for certain unpredictable reasons, such as electricity blackout.

The opening of borders has the effect of eliminating customs duties, which leads to a decrease in the price of the final product.

(XVII). TO PUT INTO CONTACT ALL THE PEOPLE FROM THE PLANET.

There are billions of people who have not travelled and seen face to face - because on TV or on the Internet we have seen - what a Chinese or an Indian looks like, how an Indian or Chinese family lives. This lack of contact creates negative myths, imaginary fears and undervalued or overvalued appreciations of certain identities. Religious radicals are convinced that atheists and agnostics are the most sinful and must be eliminated. What the radical and ultra

70

religious groups do not know is that speaking against God is not a sin, the people have a legal and moral right to test the logic of God's laws and ideas, it is not a sin to research; sometimes sins are unavoidable; sometimes love doesn't exist anymore and you simply can't live with the same person. Radicals and ultra religious and LBGT+ people can shake their hands and walk freely on the streets from Paris to Bucharest, from Berlin to London, from New York to Alaska, from Buenos Aires to Shanghai etc.

Moreover, if the radicals and ultra religious people want to talk to LGBTQ+ people, they will notice that LGBTQ+ is not the evil on Earth, the children of the devil. They are people like them, with habits and preferences, they have dreams, ideas for a better society. The only major difference is the love between people of the same sex. That's it.

In the world state, the fear of the foreigner can be eliminated, negative myths and imaginary fears can disappear, hatred of race and sexual orientation can be eliminated, and appreciation can become realistic and balanced.

A strategy that can facilitate the achievement of such a goal is communication: today it is not done enough and positively, so as to diminish at a faster and more advanced level the inheritance of

the negative context about other identities.
At the same time, today there is a false
discourse created around the idea of
community. For example, many countries
(generally in Eastern and Southern Europe,
the Middle East, Africa, Latin America, Asia)
talk about protecting life and promise to
create a more effective system, but there are
videos that show a disturbing contradiction
of 'peaceful methods' of help where, for
example, women and children are subjected
to a persistent system of physical and sexual
abuse known and ignored by the
authorities. A world state with the same
laws, rewards and sanctions can put an end
to these acts which can never be justified.

Another subject included in this goal is
marriage. Love has no borders and is
essentially multi-colored, but nevertheless
there are borders created at the heart of
local and regional traditions. Quite simply,
people are educated from the first minutes
of their life that the best choice of love is
when the other half is part of the same value
system in which they were born. There is
nothing wrong to follow native and local
traditions, but it is wrong to impose limits
on love. A neutral ground must be found
and accepted where both partners can enjoy
the spontaneously developed love without
worrying about the opinion of parents and
other community members, and where an
interest in the spirit of the loved one is more

important than a dance in the middle of the night around the fire, or wearing a folk costume only on a certain day of the year. A world state can protect a new kind of family where different local beliefs and customs can intertwine in peace and safety.

(XVIII). COOPERATION WITH DIFFERENT IDENTITIES IN ALL AREAS OF HUMAN ACTIVITY:

biology, automotive engineering, physics, geography, history and so on; between homosexuals, heterosexuals, followers and agnostics, and so on. There are many people who can work and have great ideas, but are rejected for reasons related to their ethnicity, sexual orientation, or country of origin. This unjust situation must be stopped forever.

(XIX). WORLD (GLOBAL) FREE MARKET.

We can sell a product anywhere in the world. For example, even in China's domestic market (now you need the government approval for any sold product) and North Korea (less accessible than China).

(XX). MOVEMENT OF CAPITAL AND INVESTMENT.[26]

Once we have a world state, one can invest much more easily and more in those poorly developed territories without encountering opposition from any authorities or criminal and terrorist organizations in that territory. It is a movement of capital and an internal investment that benefits all citizens.

(XXI). A SINGLE CURRENCY.[27]

A currency in every continent makes human life more interesting. The issue of currency value and conversion remains. Some currencies will be stronger and more valuable than others. With some currencies we will be able to buy more products in other territories, with other currencies less. It will be necessary to maintain a close value or if not, the currency should be valuable enough to allow access to basic needs, to ensure a better life compared to present, for

---

[26] Robert Keohane and Joseph S. Nye, *Putere și interdependență*, traducere Adriana Straub (Iași: Editura Polirom, 2009): 292; Fariborz Moshirian, "The Significance of a World Government," 1436.

[27] For a single currency see Richard N. Cooper, "A Monetary System for the Future," *Foreign Affairs* 63 (1984): 177, accessed September 2015, https://www.foreignaffairs.com/articles/1984-09-01/monetary-system-future.

example not to move for benefits from one
country to another, not to cause migratory
waves of tens and hundreds of thousands of
people in other territories, thus advancing a
pressure on the budget of another territory
(most of the time it creates a bad image
about the migrants in the new society and
can exist for centuries; rarely, it can lead to
civil conflicts for long term). However, the
choice of a continental currency is a reason
for a long term dispute between the most
powerful countries in the continent, for
example in Europe Great Britain wants to
keep the pound sterling, the countries of the
euro zone also want to keep the euro, and,
of course, Russia wants the Russian ruble.

One currency is good because there will
be no more problems with the value of the
currency and the conversion system.
Richard N. Cooper in the article *A Monetary
System for the Future* -in fact one of the
sources of inspiration for conspiracy
articles in the cyberspace-, wrote that
"Exchange rates are more credibly fixed if
they are eliminated all together, if,
international transactions, take place under
one currency," but, Cooper writes, "it is only
possible under one monetary system (see
goal *(V). ONE SYSTEM OF LAWS FOR ALL
FIELDS OF HUMAN ACTIVITY*) and one
authority issuing the currency of the state

and which directs monetary policies."[28] Today some currencies are worth more, others very little. Being a single currency, there will be no need to go to work in another country because the currency there is more valuable than ours.

Moreover, the same value of the currency can be established wherever we are, and the effect would be welcome: the number of products bought in Bulgaria would be the same as the number of products bought in the Philippines or in Peru. A single currency can lead to (I) the equalisation of the wage amount and (II) the equal value of the wage across the planet. A single currency on Earth will simplify people's lives and the economic environment.

(XXII). MOVEMENT OF IDEAS, INFORMATION AND SCIENTIFIC KNOWLEDGE WORLDWIDE.[29]

Nowadays, scientific ideas and knowledge are available to people who have access to a library and the Internet, but are citizens of certain countries that do not have access to these basic, yet, highly important services. Moreover, access to real science is

---

[28] *Ibidem*, 177.
[29] Robert Keohane and Joseph S. Nye, *Putere și interdependență*, 293.

accessible only to those countries with a good economy, because science costs money.

Due to lack of funds, many countries cannot afford access to ideas and scientific knowledge. They are isolated. The world state will be obliged to ensure access to scientific information for the population and for those countries that today and tomorrow cannot afford it. All Earth's population will have access to the latest scientific discoveries. Who can say that the discovery of a new medical treatment or a new theory can only be made by an American or a Swiss? What if a Somali man, once he has access to scientific data, reads lots of research papers in International Relations, discovers the grand theory that International Relations theorists are looking for? I am from Romania, I accessed scientific databases from Romania, England, Poland and Slovakia and I wrote this digital book: there is no research papers that gathers together and explores *in-extenso* the positive goals of the world state; it was possible because there is freedom of travel between EU member countries and I had free access to libraries and internet in four countries.

Once the borders are open, people will make contact and ideas and knowledge will be transmitted between them. A world state allows a movement of political, social,

economic, cultural, ecological and religious
ideas at a level never seen before.

(XXIII). LIFE OPPORTUNITIES.[30]

(I) Tourism across the planet without visa
in countries that now are isolated as North
Korea, or caught in conflicts and civil wars,
as the Palestinian Authority with Israel,
Egypt, Syria and so forth. We can admire the
mountains in China, the Grand Canyon in
the USA, and natural reserves in Africa
within 72 hours.

(II) We can make contact more easily and
quickly with other humans, cultures and
traditions from Europe, Africa, Asia, Latin
America etc.

(III) Access to jobs anywhere in the world.
We are going on a trip, we love the area, we
want to stay longer, apply for a job, if we are
good in our field, jobs are available, we can
work. We will not have to obtain a work
permit from the territorial authority, as it
happens today in all countries, except for
EU countries. We will not be rejected on the
grounds that we are not a citizen of the

---

[30] Ronald Tinnevelt, "Federal World Government," 231
quotes Luis Cabrera, *Political Theory of Global Justice. A
Cosmopolitan Case for the World State*, (London, New York:
Routledge, 2004): 4, book consulted by author.

country, the job will be won by the best of a Chinese, Moroccan, Thai, Cambodian or Bulgarian, or, better said, by the best candidate.

(IV) To present our personal ideas to the entire planet; we can attend conferences in any field in any current countries more easily, the passport and visa is eliminated.

(V) To establish wherever we want without having to get married to a citizen of that territory.

(VI) To marry anywhere we want and with whom we want: woman-man, man-man, woman-woman.

(XXIV). THE WORLDWIDE DISTRIBUTION OF THE ECONOMIC PRODUCT.

The world state eliminates customs duties, which makes the final product cheaper and accessible to all citizens. In addition, there will be no need to send an application to each former national state in order to approve a product which must meet certain requirements (today the requirements are different from country to country). Being a single state, therefore a single government and institutional model of operation, a product accepted by the USA authorities can be sold without any changes in content and instructions directly on the economic market in Egypt.

(XXV). TO PROVIDE BASIC NEEDS.[31]

Currently, there are countries whose population is suffering from starvation. In the world state, by the fact that we all become citizens of the same state, is obliged to provide the basic needs: food, shelter, medical services and physical security. The fulfilment of these needs can be made much easier by opening the borders (it allows the movement of capital and investments, i.e. it creates jobs; the agricultural areas in today's countries, but undeveloped due to lack of capital, can be developed); by expanding companies (creates jobs); through tourism (construction of hotels, guesthouses); by expanding the market of products and consumption; by dividing and sharing in a sustainable method the natural resources and population management.

(XXVI). TO REDUCE OR EVEN TO ELIMINATE POVERTY.

---

[31] Ronald Tinnevelt, "Federal World Government," 231; Luis Cabrera, *Political Theory of Global Justice,* 4.

The movement of capital, investments and access through tourism in today's countries with a rich, but isolated culture, in economically poorly developed areas, helps to create jobs, which means reducing and even eliminating poverty.

One of the greatest challenge of the world state is to find solutions (I) for areas where the population does not want to move due to existence of a traditional heritage of the place where they were born; (II) for areas where there are serious and hard to address negative effects of the climate change that endangers the survival of the inhabitants; (III) finally, to deal with the lack of confidence of businesses for the economic development of an area prone to an ecological disaster. In this case, the only good long-term solution is to relocate the population to a better area, or to grant to inhabitants the right to decide their destiny, where the institution of the world state is not promoted as the culprit for the independent choices of the inhabitants and the final results of the climate change.

(XXVII). TO END THE STRUGGLE FOR POWER BETWEEN COUNTRIES.[32]

---

[32] Herbert W. Brigs, "World Government and the Control of Atomic Energy," *Annals of the American Academy of Political and Social Science* 249, (1947): 46, accessed February 10, 2015,

Because there will be only one state, a competitor is automatically eliminated which means the world state cannot continue the traditional struggle for survival and supremacy. Of course, the world state will fight for the survival of all people on the planet (for access to basic human needs; in the world state, work in agriculture and in all other fields will continue). In the world state there will be a fight between political parties[33], but in the fight the political parties will not use nuclear and biological bombs, grenades, tanks, tens of thousands of soldiers and thousands of dead, terrorist attacks, a political agenda against a specific group to create a wave of negative emotion to encourage people to vote them, but win-win results, consensus, pacifist ideas and projects.

(XXVIII). TO END THE STRUGGLE FOR TERRITORIAL CONQUEST.[34]

Since the world state will become one country, it will be the home of all the people on Earth, it will own everything, and people who today fight to have a territory of their own, a home of their own (for example the

---

http://www.jstor.org/stable/1025423.

[33] *Ibidem,* 46.

[34] Dante, *The Banquet* (*Il Convito*), 103.

82

Palestinians, the Israelis, the Kurds from parts of Turkey and Syria), they will not do it anymore, they have no reason. Today's countries will no longer pursue certain strategic territories to improve their geopolitical power and for natural resources; there is no longer a plausible and justified reason for a strategic geographical area to provide an advantage in the fight against others. Planet Earth is everyone's country, everyone's resources. Dante wrote in *The Banquet*:

> *„But since the human mind in restricted possession of the Earth finds no peace, but always desires to acquire Glory, as we see by experience, discords and wars must arise between realm and realm [...] Wherefore, in order to prevent these wars, and to remove the causes of them through all the Earth, so far as it is given to the Human Race to possess it, there must of necessity be Monarchy, that is to say, one sole principality; and there must be one Prince,*

83

*who, possessing all, and
not being able to desire
more, holds the Kings
content within the limits of
the kingdoms, so that
peace may be between
them [...] may dwell
together in mutual love; in
this love the houses obtain
all they need, which, being
obtained, men can live
happily, which is that end
for which man was born
[...]."[35]*

(XXIX). TO ELIMINATE THE WAR OF ALL AGAINST ALL.[36]

Because there will be a single state that owns the whole Earth (recognizes all identities, education, offers the same rights and obligations for all, it's a common society), there will be no reason why we should resort to war.

---

[35] Dante, *The Banquet*, 103.
[36] 'Bellum omnium contra omnes.' It means to get out from Thomas Hobbes din *De Cive* and Leviathan world. Campbell Craig, "The Resurgent Idea," 142; Herbert W. Brigs, "World Government," 42, 45-46; Alexander Wendt, "Why a World State," 502, 522, 528. Luis Cabrera, "Global Government," 474-475.

The elimination of wars appears in second two after the emergence of the world state. Likewise, all current countries and ethnic groups within countries are losing the ability to make voluntary war. Religious and ethnic cleansing wars are eliminated. Eliminates instantly the threats with a nuclear holocaust.[37] The arms market will disappear; being a single state, it will have legal authority in all territories[38], and there is no need for arms market because there will be no more enemies who want to steal other people's territory and resources.

A positive effect of this change is the budget: the investments[39] for the human agency in the army and the creation of hard weapons will be massively reduced: there is no need for machine guns, grenades, tanks, war planes, war ships, war helicopters, bombs (biological, chemical, nuclear) etc. Instead, a larger budget can be allocated to education, culture, tourism, the business environment etc.

Of course, the one common point, probably shared by the entire population of the planet, is the existence of an army and weaponry ready to fight against a possible

---

[37] James A. Yunker, "Evolutionary World Government," 96; Luis Cabrera, "Global Government," 476.

[38] See Lincoln P. Bloomfield, "Arms Control and World Government," *World Politics* 14 (1962): 633-645, accessed February 10, 2015, doi: 10.2307/2009312.

[39] Shmuel Nili, "Who's Afraid," 246.

attack from extraterrestrial space (either
from another species, or the destruction of
otherwise unstoppable meteorites which
can endanger the survival of the humans).

(xxx). ONE ARMY.

The construction of a world army per se is
not necessary, but it can exist as a symbol of
the existence of a single world state and
because it is an element of the state:
security and defence. Since the world state
will be recognized by current countries and
their population, the army of current
countries will form the army of the world
state; it can be named Earth Army?
However, the armies of current countries
will not be relocated to another territory,
but will remain in the territory they were in
before the world state. Local authorities will
have the same role: to continue to apply the
law in villages and towns, but with a
worldwide vision.

However, there will be a massive
difference: in the world state the
phenomenon of 'enemy countries' and
'friendly countries'[40] is lost forever and,
therefore, there will no longer be an army

---

[40] I use 'phenomenon' because of the ever changing nature
of the relations between countries: treaties (of any nature)
can create a new friend and at the same time a new enemy.

for war and defence. In other words, the basic function is changed: to support the population before and after ecological disasters, or other events that can be solved through a high number of specific and specialized groups of people.

(XXXI). TO ELIMINATE TERRORISM.[41]

Global citizenship, identical educational system, the recognition of all identities, the end of the struggle for territorial conquest to have a home or for natural resources, in time will eliminate terrorism.

(XXXII). TO ELIMINATE CORRUPTION.

Many states are corrupt because of the personality of the people, their historical evolution and the forms of government and the religious system, in other words, corruption exists in all states of the world, from poor countries to rich and technologically advanced countries.

Since the world state is able to provide basic needs, a unique educational system and political stability, people will no longer have to look for solutions considered to be an act of corruption in order to survive

---

[41] Luis Cabrera, "Global Government," 475.

decently. However, corruption will not disappear permanently, in the sense that official reports will score corruption 0 - although in time it could exist; people will still try to trick people and the laws, but the level of corruption will be significantly reduced. It will no longer be possible to commit so many and intense illegalities as to endanger the future of the entire world state, therefore of the entire human species.

(XXXIII). TO ELIMINATE ORGANIZED CRIME.

And here, since the world state can provide the basic needs, people will no longer be inclined to fight for financial benefits, and as a method to turn to voluntary and involuntary prostitution, drug trafficking and other substances harmful to humans, animals and rare plants on the black market.

(XXXIV). TO ENSURE THE SECURITY OF ALL HUMAN IDENTITIES.[42]

Learning the truth through education, that is, all people are equal regardless of race, culture, language, religion, sexual

---

[42] Fariborz Moshirian, "The Significance of a World Government," 1436.

orientation, is going to help people to understand those who are different, because after all, they are also different from others. Every identity has the right to walk freely at any time on all of the streets of villages and cities, even in parks and forests without CCTVs to capture each second of our life; the population must live in a safe environment without brutal interventions in the narrative line.

(XXXV). TO DIMINISH AND EVEN ELIMINATE THE HATRED BETWEEN HUMAN RACES.

An educational system oriented towards promoting equality among people and creating a system of civilizational orientation and tolerance towards all races, cultures, languages, religions, sexual orientations, will help people to understand those who are different, because after all, they are also different of others. At the end of the day, every individual deserves to sleep with peace of mind that it was a great day and individual personality matters and it is valued by the community.

(XXXVI). TO DIMINISH AND EVEN ELIMINATE THE HATRED BETWEEN SEXUAL ORIENTATIONS.

89

In the last twenty years the transgender social movement has become widely known in the online environment and in the public space. The main idea is to accept people whose gender identity or gender expression does not correspond with their sex assigned at birth; at the other side of this state of nature, are people with a strong feeling of not belonging in the right body and want to change their biological sex, want to have the right to decide the need of a sex reassignment surgery to be able to align at an advance level their primary and secondary sex characteristics with their gender identity[43].

At the same time, there are people who feel that they do not fit into the traditional binomial of woman or man; in order to live the transgender state of nature, the transgender movement demands the right to be respected for their given-by-nature lifestyle and to have access to the medical system that can make possible the change they want and need, and without being discriminated against by state institutions, companies, public persons, etc, for personal choice.

The transgender movement is right: transgender people have the right to decide the course of their lives and their choice

---

[43] Wikipedia, *Transgender*, available at: https://en.wikipedia.org/wiki/Transgender, last accessed: October 1, 2022.

must be respected; the world state can provide the transgender movement with their truth through education, namely that all people are equal regardless of race, gender, culture, language, religion, sexual orientation; the world state can help the people to understand those who are different, because after all, they are also different from others.

(XXXVII). TO SAVE HUMAN SPECIES FROM SELF-DESTRUCTION.[44]

The great misunderstandings of humanity have roots in the religious set of ideas, the racial superiority, the biological set of sexual orientations and genders, lack of natural resources, etc. All this generates a conflictual situation.

In the past, racial superiority, non-recognition of the other's identity and the struggle for power brought the Jewish holocaust, the Armenian genocide of 1894-1896/1915-1916, the Rwandan genocide of 1994, religious and ethnic terrorists. In 1990, it was believed that after the fall of the USSR, the world would become a safer

---

[44] Yael Tamil, "Who's Afraid of a Global State?" in *Nationalism and Internationalism in the Post-Cold War Era*, ed. Kjell Goldmann et al. (London, New York: Routledge, 2000): 260; Hans J. Morgenthau, *Politica între naţiuni,* 517; Richard Little, "Şcoala engleză vs realismul american," 625.

place, but, surprisingly, the world has become even more unsafe.

The struggle for identity recognition and survival continues. There is a greater chance today than in the past, that a new nuclear holocaust, ethnic genocide or world war to occur. In 2012, The Doomsday Clock - is a design in the form of an internationally recognized symbolic clock, which shows how many minutes separate humanity from a catastrophe of global proportions -, showed 5 minutes to midnight[45]; in 2015, because of the events in Ukraine from 2013-2015, in which the USA, the European Union and Russia were involved, the clock showed 3 minutes to midnight (this time also existed in 1949 when the USSR tested the first nuclear weapons and in 1984 during the arms race between the USA and the USSR).

In January 2022 the clock showed 1 minute and 40 seconds to midnight[46], and, at last check on October 1, 2022, the clock showed the same time as in January 2022.

It is well known that humans, for recognition and survival, are willing to act with the most inappropriate tools.

---

[45] "Timeline," Bulletin of the Atomic Scientists, accessed November 5, 2015, http://thebulletin.org/timeline.
[46] John Mecklin, "At doom's doorstep: It is 100 seconds to midnight", *Bulletin of the Atomic Scientists*, available at: https://thebulletin.org/doomsday-clock/current-time/, last accessed: October 1, 2022.

One state for all the Earth's population is the only solution to turn back the clock, to save us from self-destruction.

(XXXVIII). TO BUILD A PEACEFUL HUMAN CONSCIOUSNESS.

This goal is tremendously difficult to achieve, probably never in full form, but much more than in present. When all identities are recognized and accepted, there is an environment where all identities feel safe, access to basic needs, we are going to be able to acknowledge and observe in front of us the path of peace between everyone.

(XXXIX). PEACEFUL CONTACT AND DIALOGUE WITH OTHER DIFFERENT IDENTITIES (RACES, CULTURES, TRADITIONS, RELIGIONS).[47]

Today, the contact with other identities is more difficult because there is a historical baggage with a negative vision towards those who are different. A single educational system for the entire population, the elimination of the cult of personality and religious wars, the recognition of all identities and access to

---

[47] Yael Tamil, "Who's Afraid," 251.

basic needs, makes possible a peaceful contact between people.

(XL). CIVILIZATIONAL ORIENTATION.[48]

Let's respect all human identities, legal rights and obligations, let the state institutions to function at full for everyone, care for the ecological environment, kindness, mutual help, individual freedom, of expression, of religion; to achieve a high level of development of human society through tolerance towards those who are different, and yet like us.

(XLI). TO LIVE IN A COMMON REALITY.

Today, some states are caught in civil wars, others live in peace. A visible number of countries and their population can afford (and happens on a daily basis) to throw food away with no care for other people and the environment. A visible number of people in other countries (Africa, Latin America) and from refugee camps (Middle East, North Africa) can survive only with the help of the UN aid convoy for humanitarian

---

[48] Christopher Chase-Dunn and Hiroko Inoue, "Accelerating Democratic Global State Formation," *Cooperation and Conflict* 47 (2012): 160, accessed May 19, 2014, doi: 10.1177/0010836712443168.

crisis, which provide free food and shelter for people in need.

A world state can build a single reality that all citizens will take advantage of: a state of peace, without wars, civil conflicts, terrorist acts; with well-being and physical security, etc.

(XLII). TO LIVE IN A COMMON SOCIETY.

We will have a society with multiple identities of the human agency. We will have the same norms and values wherever we walk on Earth. We will all be different, and we will all be members of one community.

(XLIII). TO HAVE A COMMON DESTINY.

A large part of the Earth's population has a destiny of isolation from other populations; a small scale of people are isolated even from their brothers and sisters, for example North Koreans: although they are the same race and speak the same language, they have no contact with South Koreans; between Romanians and Moldovans there is a weak contact, and gets worse especially when the struggle for power and national identity is more important on the politicians' agenda. The LGBT+ community has a destiny of rejection even by parents, brothers and sisters. Women and children have a destiny of abuse. Men, in the name of the survival of the family, keeping alive the long term family customs and for the existence of the society, have to sacrifice their own life and face and doing the high risks jobs, such as soldier on the battlefield: ready to die for the greater good. The "proportion of people living on less than $5.50 per day, globally is 43%, while the proportion of people living on less than $3.20 per day, globally is 24%"[49].

In some countries, the life expectancy is lower, in other countries higher; this situation is because of the living conditions: for the population of a country without agriculture or with a poorly developed agricultural system, a corrupt and unproductive educational and medical system, surrounded by ethnic and religious conflicts, the life expectancy is lower.

Some people have a destiny of struggles for identity recognition and survival. Some people, for survival, become assassins and drug dealers, they have a destiny of criminal activity. In the world state, those populations that today live on average 45-

---

[49] Zach Christensen, Dan Walton, 'Poverty trends: global, regional and national', *Development Initiatives*, November 10, 2022, available at: https://devinit.org/resources/poverty-trends-global-regional-and-national/, last accessed: October 1, 2022.

50 years, will be able to live longer, certainly 60-70 years. In time, the average life of a human being can be between 80-90 years, maybe even 90-100 years. Surely more people than today will get to live over a hundred years.

In the world state, we will all have the same destiny offered by the state: peace, rights for all, long life, well-being and physical security. As for individual destiny, as it happens today in those countries that have a destiny of peace and well-being, some citizens will be mathematicians, others biologists, journalists, factory workers etc.

(XLIV). MORAL AND SPIRITUAL PROGRESS.[50]

The elimination of terrorism, of all wars, religion in intimate space, the existence of a common reality and society is going to contribute enormously to the moral and spiritual evolution of the humans. Lack of negative actions against others help to create a positive spirit ready to be noticed by others and shared by most people.

---

[50] Yael Tamil, "Who's Afraid," 251; Ronald Tinnevelt, "Federal World Government," 220.

(XLV). TO LEAVE THE ANARCHIC WORLD.[51]

In world state we leave the world of anarchy (I) in the sense of chaos and conflict for power, territorial conquests, natural resources and (II) in the sense of the emergence of a strong central government that will apply one system of laws for all current countries and their citizens.

(XLVI). TO CREATE A WORLD ORDER.[52]

A world state builds a new world order, namely all countries will agree with laws, theories and methods that are good for humanity. This new world order is going to create stability and principles to help the humanity to continue its existence on planet Earth.

(XLVII). SOLIDARITY BETWEEN DIFFERENT HUMAN IDENTITIES.[53]

---

[51] Joshua Goldstein şi Jon C. Pevehouse, *Relaţii Internaţionale*, traducere Andreea-Ioana Cozianu, Elena Farca şi Adriana Straub (Iaşi: Editura Polirom, 2008): 108.
[52] Campbell Craig, "The Resurgent Idea," 142; Yael Tamil, "Who's Afraid," 259.
[53] Ronald Tinnevelt, "Federal World Government," 232.

In the world state all human races will have the same responsibilities and common interests, such as to avoid a new world war and to care about the needs of others, to help an identity different from our own. Solidarity with our fellows neighbours helps the spirit to progress to a level unheard and unknown by a visible number of people across the planet.

(XLVIII). TO BUILD AND TO MAINTAIN TOGETHER A PEACEFUL WORLD STATE.[54]

Every citizen can contribute to the development of the world state, and that is precisely why we need to know as much information as possible about the effectiveness of a world state and how willing we are to support such a project.

Maintaining a pacifist world state must meet two conditions: (I) routine and (II) consistency in the application of laws and citizens' expectations of the world state. These conditions must be followed by citizens, and enforced and monitored by local authorities on a daily basis.

---

[54] Hans J. Morgenthau, *Politica între naţiuni,* 527; Ronald Tinnevelt, "Federal World Government," 224; Fariborz Moshirian, "The Significance of a World Government," 1436.

(XLIX). TO LIVE TOGETHER.

A beautiful and advanced image of the human spirit is when we are walking down the street and a person, with a different identity than ours, looks at us and smiles, and we feel the joy of receiving a positive sign from another member of the community, and in return we smile too. And let this image be available in every corner of the world and as often as possible every day, for everyone.

(L). SOCIALISATION.

This goal was said and written by Immanuel Kant in *Începutul şi sfârşitul (The Begining and the End)* "socialisation - the ultimate goal of humans."[55] But this socialisation, in full form and much improved from today, can be obtained only in a world state.

World state, by achieving certain goals, such as (I), (II), (III), (IV), (V), (VI), (VII), (VIII), (X), (XIII) (XIV), (XV) and (XVII) helps to create socialisation between different human identities, but peacefully: it will transmit knowledge, traditions and values among all people in the world. From each identity we can learn something good:

---

[55] Immanuel Kant, *Începutul şi sfârşitul, (The Begining and the End)*, (Bucureşti, Editura All: 2011):11, electronic edition.

from atheists, agnostics, Christians, Muslims, Buddhists, white, black, homosexual and so forth. Muslims, Christians and atheists can meet at conferences to discuss the existence of divinity without bombs and negative feelings before and after the meeting, because killing or hurting a human who wants and has a different life from ours means moral regress. A world state offers the chance for the first time in the human history -for all citizens and future-citizen, *that the animal human to become a human being.*

This goal is best achieved by protecting the new type of family that has emerged as a result of the unification of the people of the planet: multi-ethnic, multi-linguistic and multi-racial. The level of socialization is going to be much richer and colorful because the new human (developed and appeared after the disappearance of the national state) will have at its genetic base several identities that interconnect and, any measure taken to support and recognize another citizen, it means a support and recognition of one's own family and identity.

4. To achieve the above goals, several requirements must be achieved. Here are four of them:

(I) all humans must obey and comply in the public space the judicial laws, because these laws provide the same rights and obligations for all humans;

(II) the belief in a deity should become intimate, individual, independent, without aggressively exposure in the lives of others and in public;

(III) the religious leaders will have to renounce to sacrifice the life and the image of humans who do not fit the profile of believer that appears in books considered divine, to not promote a religious cult as the sole and final truth of this world;

(IV) political leaders will have to renounce to sacrifice racial, religious and sexual orientation minorities to be elected for a public office, for example a candidate makes a campaign with Christian or Muslim identity, because in that city are living more Christians or Muslims; the candidate is presenting the electoral campaign as a victim: "I'm and I feel discriminated because I'm Christian or Muslim;" all political leaders must address the public on the following idea: "I'm the candidate of all; I fight to defend the rights of all identities in this village or city; no one will be left behind."

102

Conclusions

1. In this research paper, I decided to go against the negative thread of the world state and **(i)** I challenged the conventional wisdom of the negative goals of the world state by exploring fifty positive goals; **(ii)** I helped to enhance the human imagination regarding the possibility of a positive end of the world state; **(iii)** I invited people to believe that the world state is good for humanity as quickly as they think it is bad for humanity; **(iv)** I provided a point of reference for curious readers looking for positive goals of the world state. The main argument of the paper is the need for a positive position to counterbalance the negative goals. In the end, I built what is missing: **(i)** a narrative line where the world state can bring advantages and benefits to humanity and **(ii)** I created a balance of the narrative line of the goals of the world state by exploring fifty positive goals.

2. The world state, although presented as a negative idea in the public and cyberspace, it is a theoretical and practical solution to solve today's major problems that we cannot ignore.

3. The goals written in this paper **(I)** are not new to the existing science of the world state, in the sense that in this paper they were described for the first time in the history of research about the world state; **(II)** are new to curious fellows who just read for the first time about the world state and negative and positive goals; **(III)** are a novelty because are gathered in a single theoretical body and explored in-extenso; I have used various sources to find several goals that provide a basic picture and exposes a truth: the goals of the world state are not a secret as claimed by the conspiracy theorists, but there is a rich and serious literature created and advanced by scholars with good intentions and real identity; however, both sides need to be researched and brought into the light, so that the general public to educate and develop a profound awareness of and mentally exercise both visions of the end of the world state; **(IV)** are a novelty because, taken together, negative and positive, form a general picture of the goals of the world state, it moves the human imagination; **(V)** until the publication of this research paper,

104

we knew more about the negative goals,
today is a new day: we also know positive
goals.

4. There are multiple positive goals and this
fact should encourage us, to have reasons
why we should help to build a world state,
so that we can then enjoy the advantages of
a human union. Certainly, the road is not
easy and rosy, but the picture around us is
real and brutal: humanity is caught in a
vicious circle of shortages, wars, hatred of
race, religion and sexual orientation. The
world state is a solution to all these
problems.

5. World state goals must be achieved
gradually, step by step, not all at once, the
process of building a world state can easily
exceed a couple of hundred of years. Indeed,
some goals, namely **(I), (II), (III), (IV),
(V), (VI), (VII), (XXIII), (XXVII), (XXVIII),
(XXIX), (XXX), (XXXVII), (XXXV),
(XXXVIII), (XLI), (XLII), (XLV)** and **(XLVI)**
will be achieved in second two after we vote
a world state, but other goals will be
achieved in time. For example, we cannot
open all borders in a day, but gradually for a
more efficient flow of people. Imagine what
could happen if today, being free to travel
around the world, the poor populations
migrate to rich countries? Or look at the
refugees from Europe produced by wars in

Ukraine and Middle East. It's a huge pressure on the budgets of european states. The integration of refugees will take years; some will never integrate into a new society. If today we open the national borders, the result will be a world catastrophe. We must first distribute and build minimal welfare in all countries, then we can open the borders. The existence of welfare in each state eliminates migration and displacement of people. Why? Because their basic needs are met. No longer have to flee to another state to survive. Although they are in the EU, Swedes have not migrated to the Netherlands, Spaniards in Italy and French in Germany. Between these countries there is a relation of peaceful cooperation, they visit each other, do not run after the conquest of the other state, they are tourists one for another. Only people from poor countries are running for survival in other states. The borders must be opened partially, for instance maximum of three months per year you can travel and work anywhere in the world. This step to be valid for five to ten years. Then to introduce six months for another five to ten years. Finally, after constructing a normal flow of human transport, the existence of a different mentality, we can get the right to freedom of travel and work anywhere and anytime on Earth, as it happens in the current countries, in the USA and in the EU.

Finally, the Earth will be more of a flow of tourists, not people seeking food and shelter. We will travel and we get to see all the places of the planet, peaceful 24/7, not just the village, town or territory where we were born. The EU began its road back in 1952. Today in 2022 we do not have a fully European state, but we are witnessing a crisis of identity. Some EU citizens want to continue the path towards a united Europe, others citizens see only the path of nationalism, or, recently, extremist nationalism.

6. The construction of a world state is laborious difficult because it needs the support of at least 51% of the planet's population, i.e. more than 3.5 billion people. A world state, in my opinion and based on today's political and human reality, will appear in the next 200 - 300 years. A functional and efficient world state will be built in about 150-200 years after we have a world state. The second result of a study by Peter N. Peregrine, Melvin Ember, and Carol R. Ember, which predicts future values of political integration, suggests that 3000 years from now, sometime in the year 5000 CE, all peoples will be incorporated into the one world state.[56] Of course, it does not

---

[56] Peter N. Peregrine, Melvin Ember and Carol R. Ember, "Predicting the Future State of the World Using

mean that we have to postpone the idea, but on the contrary, to hurry it up, to enjoy as soon as possible the intercontinental journeys with only an identity card, a world without wars, let us come into peaceful contact with different races, cultures, traditions, etc. Why we should not enjoy free access to all inhabited and uninhabited areas of the planet?

7. World state is a subject on which each Earth citizen must contribute according with their abilities, either through a deeper understanding of the benefits and risks completed through personal research, or with theoretical interventions in all the fields of the human activity that can make the world state a reality. The best advice I have is to not wait for political, religious leaders and websites with hidden administrators, to tell us what to do and what to believe about the world state. It is time to take the idea of a world state into our hands and process it inside our minds, to show our faces, to share our thinking with everyone at any point we feel the need to explore it as another solution to the current system of power politics and lifestyle.

Archaeological Data: An Exercise in Archaeomancy," *Cross-Cultural Research* 38 (2004): 133,144, accessed January 7, 2015, doi: 10.1177/1069397103260510.

8. Like it or not, the world state must become one of the main concerns of the people, because *we, the people* decide what the world looks like tomorrow. The world state is not made by conquest and imposition, but voluntarily by people. Alexander Wendt noted in 2005 that "human beings dictate the speed of formation and the character of the world state."[57] But the voluntary approach must be based on a generous level of information about the possibilities of building a real and worthy world state, including even negative expectations. Ignoring a possible project, even theoretically, is life-threatening for the continuation of today's society.

Many times in the history of the world, politicians and artists from all fields of study have abandoned theoretical plans on the grounds that they do not reflect reality, because the plans were a little bit or too much on an utopian tone. And many times there was a visible and unpardonable regret for not trying an idea, a less realistic and more utopian project. Today is the historic chance to try and implement an idealistic plan. A chance to build a new world order: all for one and one for all. The present generation was born in anarchy,

[57] Alexander Wendt, "Agency, Teleology and the World State: A Reply to Shannon," *European Journal of International Relations* 11 (2005): 597, accessed May 19, 2014, doi: 10.1177/1354066105057903.

poverty, wars, famine, etc. The present generation can make future generations to be born and to enjoy the life in a world of order and well-being. We no longer have to postpone the idea, we no longer have to find excuses. Each of us must participate to build the world state. If not today, then when? After a lunatic leader in search for power and personal prestige, a terrorist group or even a state, because its sovereignty is violated, drops a nuclear or biological bomb destroying large parts of the environment? We can avoid such a scenario. We can test the idea of the world state in practice. Let's see if it's good or bad. Today, more than ever in the history of the world, we have the chance to unite under one sky and one nation. I end the research paper with a proposal and a question for all the people of planet Earth: "let us lay aside every weight, and the sin which doth so easily beset us, and let us run with patience the race that is set before us" (Hebrew 12:1); can we live together?

BIBLIOGRAPHY

Books:

1. Aligheri, Dante. *De Monarchia*. 1309-1913. Accessed November 3, 2015. http://oll.libertyfund.org/titles/2196.
2. Aligheri, Dante. *The Banquet*. (1304-1306). Accessed November 3, 2015. http://www.gutenberg.org/ebooks/12867.
3. Cabrera, Luis. *Political Theory of Global Justice. A Cosmopolitan Case for the World State*. London, New York: Routledge, 2004.
4. Goldstein, Joshua S. and Pevehouse, Jon C. *Relaţii Internaţionale*. Iaşi: Editura Polirom, 2008.
5. Hagger, Nicholas. *The World Government: A Blueprint for a Universal World State* . Washington: O-Books, 2010.
6. Jackson, Robert H. and Georg Sørensen. *Introduction to International Relations: Theories and Approaches*, Fifth Edition. London, New York: Oxford University Press, 2013.
7. Kant, Immanuel. *Idea for a Universal History with a Cosmopolitan Purpose*. (1784). Accessed November 3, 2015. https://www.marxists.org/reference/subject/ethics/kant/universal-history.htm,
8. Kant, Immanuel. *Începutul şi sfârşitul*. Bucureşti, Editura All, 2011. Electronic edition.

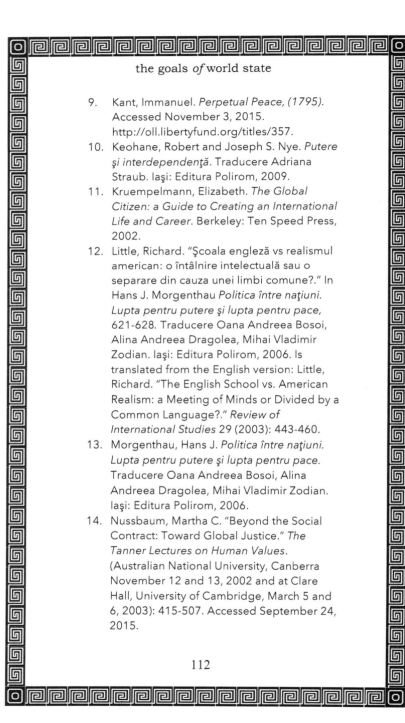

the goals *of* world state

9. Kant, Immanuel. *Perpetual Peace, (1795)*. Accessed November 3, 2015. http://oll.libertyfund.org/titles/357.
10. Keohane, Robert and Joseph S. Nye. *Putere şi interdependenţă*. Traducere Adriana Straub. Iaşi: Editura Polirom, 2009.
11. Kruempelmann, Elizabeth. *The Global Citizen: a Guide to Creating an International Life and Career*. Berkeley: Ten Speed Press, 2002.
12. Little, Richard. "Şcoala engleză vs realismul american: o întâlnire intelectuală sau o separare din cauza unei limbi comune?." In Hans J. Morgenthau *Politica între naţiuni. Lupta pentru putere şi lupta pentru pace*, 621-628. Traducere Oana Andreea Bosoi, Alina Andreea Dragolea, Mihai Vladimir Zodian. Iaşi: Editura Polirom, 2006. Is translated from the English version: Little, Richard. "The English School vs. American Realism: a Meeting of Minds or Divided by a Common Language?." *Review of International Studies* 29 (2003): 443-460.
13. Morgenthau, Hans J. *Politica între naţiuni. Lupta pentru putere şi lupta pentru pace*. Traducere Oana Andreea Bosoi, Alina Andreea Dragolea, Mihai Vladimir Zodian. Iaşi: Editura Polirom, 2006.
14. Nussbaum, Martha C. "Beyond the Social Contract: Toward Global Justice." *The Tanner Lectures on Human Values*. (Australian National University, Canberra November 12 and 13, 2002 and at Clare Hall, University of Cambridge, March 5 and 6, 2003): 415-507. Accessed September 24, 2015.

http://tannerlectures.utah.edu/_documents/
a-to-z/n/nussbaum_2003.pdf.

15. Rousseau, Jean-Jacques. *The Social
    Contract Or Principles of Political Right*.
    (1762). Accessed July 4, 2015.
    https://www.marxists.org/reference/subject/
    economics/rousseau/social-
    contract/index.htm. Electronic edition.

16. Serebrian, Oleg. *Dicţionar de geopolitică*.
    Iaşi: Editura Polirom, 2006.

17. Tamil, Yael. "Who's Afraid of a Global
    State?" In *Nationalism and Internationalism
    in the Post-Cold War Era*, edited by Kjell
    Goldmann, Ulf Hannerz and Charles Westin,
    244-265. London, New York: Routledge,
    2000.

JOURNAL ARTICLES:

1. Bloomfield, Lincoln P. "Arms Control and
   World Government." *World Politics* 14
   (1962): 633-645. Accessed February 10,
   2015. doi: 10.2307/2009312.

2. Brigs, Herbert W. "World Government and
   the Control of Atomic Energy." *Annals of the
   American Academy of Political and Social
   Science* 249 (1947): 45-53. Accessed
   February 10, 2015.
   http://www.jstor.org/stable/1025423.

3. Brigs, Herbert W. "The Problem of World
   Government." *The American Journal of
   International Law* 41 (1947): 108-112.
   Accessed February 10, 2015.
   http://www.jstor.org/stable/2193858.

4. Cabrera, Luis. "World Government:
   Renewed Debate, Persistent Challenges."

the goals *of* world state

European Journal of International Relations
16 (2010): 511-530. Accessed May 19, 2015.
doi: 10.1177/1354066109346888.

5. Cabrera, Luis. "Global Government and the
    Sources of Globoscepticism." *Millenium:*
    Journal of International Studies 43 (2015):
    471-491. Accessed January 28, 2015. doi:
    10.1177/0305829814541833.

6. Carneiro, Robert L. "The Political Unification
    of the World: Whether, When, and How -
    Some Speculations." *Cross-Cultural*
    Research 38 (2004): 162-177. Accessed
    September 3, 2015. doi:
    10.1177/1069397103260530.

7. Chase-Dunn, Christopher and Hiroko Inoue.
    "Accelerating Democratic Global State
    Formation." *Cooperation and Conflict* 47
    (2012): 157-175. Accessed May 19, 2014.
    doi: 10.1177/0010836712443168.

8. Cook, Thomas I. "Theoretical Foundations of
    World Government." *The Review of Politics*
    12 (1950): 20-55. Accessed January 7, 2015.
    doi: 10.1017/S003467050004571X.

9. Cooper, Richard N. "A Monetary System for
    the Future." *Foreign Affairs* 63 (1984): 166-
    184. Accessed September 2015.
    https://www.foreignaffairs.com/articles/198
    4-09-01/monetary-system-future.

10. Craig, Campbell. "The Resurgent Idea of
    World Government." *Ethics & International*
    Affairs 22 (2008): 133-142. Accessed
    February 10, 2015. doi: 10.1111/j.1747-
    7093.2008.00139.x.

11. Dunn, Frederick S. "The Scope of
    International Relations." *World Politics* 1
    (1948): 142-146. Accessed December 22,
    2012. doi: 10.2307/2009164.

12. Gosepath, Stefan. "The Global Scope of Justice." *Metaphilosophy* 32 (2001):135-159. Accessed September 5, 2015. doi: 10.1111/1467-9973.00179.

13. Koenig-Archibugi, Mathias. "Is Global Democracy Possible?." *European Journal of International Relations* 17 (2010): 519-542. Accessed May 19, 2014. doi: 10.1177/1354066110366056.

14. Kurth, James. "Things to Come. The Shape of the New World Order." *The National Interest* 23 (1991): 3-12. Accessed January 7, 2015. http://www.jstor.org/stable/42894742.

15. Lloyd, Wm. Bross Jr. "The United Nations and the World Federalism." *The Antioch Review* 9 (1949): 16-28. Accessed February 10, 2015. http://www.jstor.org/stable/4609313.

16. Moshirian, Fariborz. "The Significance of a World Government in the Process of Globalisation in the 21st Century." *Journal of Banking & Finance* 32 (2008): 1432-1439. Accessed September 5, 2015. doi:10.1016/j.jbankfin.2008.03.004.

17. Nili, Shmuel. "Who's Afraid of a World State? A Global Sovereign and the Statist-Cosmopolitan Debate." *Critical Review of International Social and Political Philosophy* 18 (2015): 241-263. Accessed September 9, 2015. doi: 10.1080/13698230.2013.850833.

18. Nussbaum, Martha C. "Beyond the Social Contract: Capabilities and Global Justice." *Oxford Development Studies* 32 (2004): 3-18. Accessed September 25, 2015. doi: 10.1080/1360081042000184093.

19. Peregrine, Peter N., Ember, Melvin and Ember Carol R. "Predicting the Future State of the World Using Archaeological Data: An Exercise in Archaeomancy." *Cross-Cultural Research* 38 (2004): 133-146. Accessed January 7, 2015. doi: 10.1177/1069397103260510.

20. Rogoff, Kenneth. "Why Not a Global Currency." *American Economic Review* 91 (2001): 243-247. Accessed September 2015. http://scholar.harvard.edu/files/rogoff/files/why_not_a_global_currency.pdf.

21. Scheuerman, William E. "Cosmopolitanism and the World State." *Review of International Studies* 40 (2014). Accessed April 17, 2014. doi: 10.1017/S0260210513000417.

22. Speer, James P. II. "Hans Morgenthau and the World State." *World Politics* 20 (1968): 207-227. http://www.jstor.org/stable/2009796 .

23. Strömbom, Lisa. "Thick recognition: Advancing Theory on Identity Change in Intractable Conflicts." *European Journal of International Relations* 20 (2014): 168-191, Accessed August 12, 2015. doi: 10.1177/1354066112439217.

24. Tinnevelt, Ronald. "Federal World Government: The Road to Peace and Justice?." *Cooperation and Conflict* 47 (2012): 220-238. Accessed May 19, 2014. doi: 10.1177/0010836712443173.

25. Wang, Hongying and James N. Rosenau. "China and Global Governance." *Asian Perspective* 33 (2009): 5-39. Accessed September 3, 2015. http://www.jstor.org/stable/42704681.

http://www.cebri.org/midia/documentos/05
.pdf.

26. Wendt, Alexander. "Why a World State is
    Inevitable?." *European Journal of
    International Relations* 9 (2003): 491-542.
    Accessed April 30, 2014.
    doi: 10.1177/135406610394001.

27. Wendt, Alexander. "Agency, Teleology and
    the World State: A Reply to Shannon."
    European Journal of International Relations
    11 (2005): 589-598. Accessed May 19, 2014.
    doi: 10.1177/1354066105057903.

28. Yunker, James A. "Evolutionary World
    Government." *Peace Research. The
    Canadian Journal of Peace and Conflict
    Studies* 44 (2012): 95-126. Accessed
    September 3, 2015.

29. Weiss, Thomas G. "What Happened to the
    Idea of World Government." *International
    Studies Quarterly* 53 (2009): 259-262.
    Accessed February 10, 2015. doi:
    10.1111/j.1468-2478.2009.00533.x.
    https://www.worldfederalistscanada.org/do
    cuments/09TWeissreWrldGovt.pdf.

WEBSITES:

1. Adachi, Ken. "The New World Order (NWO).
   An Overview." *The Forbidden Knowledge.*
   Last accessed November 27, 2015.
   http://educate-yourself.org/nwo/.

2. Bulletin of the Atomic Scientists, "Timeline."
   Accessed November 5, 2015.
   http://thebulletin.org/timeline.

3. "Carta Organizaţiei Naţiunilor Unite, din 26
   iunie 1945." Last accessed December 3,

2015.
http://www.anr.gov.ro/docs/legislatie/intern
ationala/Carta_Organizatiei_Natiunilor_Unit
e_ONU_.pdf.

4. Christensen, Zach. Walton, Dan. 'Poverty
trends: global, regional and national',
Development Initiatives, November 10,
2022, available at:
https://devinit.org/resources/poverty-
trends-global-regional-and-national/, last
accessed: October 1, 2022.

5. Coleman, John. "21 Goals of the Illuminati
and The Committee of 300." *Educate-
Yourself*. Last accessed December 23, 2015.
http://educate-
yourself.org/cn/johncolemangoalsofIllumina
ti.shtml.

6. Dex.ro. "Cosmopolitism." Accessed October
21, 2015. http://www.dex.ro/cosmopolitism.

7. Dictionary.reference.com.
"Cosmopolitanism." Accessed October 23,
2015.
http://dictionary.reference.com/browse/cos
mopolitanism.

8. Dexonline.ro. "Scop." Accessed October 21,
2015. https://dexonline.ro/definitie/scop.

9. Dictionary.reference.com. "Scope."
Accessed October 21, 2015.
http://dictionary.reference.com/browse/sco
pe.

10. Dictionary.reference.com. "Goal." Accessed
October 21, 2015.
http://dictionary.reference.com/browse/goa
l.

11. Faux, Jeff. "Toward a Global Social
Contract." *Economic Policy Institute*.
Accessed October 4, 2015.

http://www.epi.org/publication/webfeatures _viewpoints_mexico_grand_bargain/.

12. Lendman, Stephen. "The True Story of the Bilderberg Group and What They May Be Planning Now. A Review of Daniel Estulin's book." *Global Research*. Last accessed December 3, 2015. http://www.globalresearch.ca/the-true-story-of-the-bilderberg-group-and-what-they-may-be-planning-now/13808.

13. Guvernul României. Ministerul Afacerilor Externe. "Coreea de Nord." Accessed November 23, 2015. http://www.mae.ro/travel-conditions/3685.

14. Neidleman, Jason. "The Social Contract Theory in a Global Context." *E-International Relations*. Accessed October 4, 2015. http://www.e-ir.info/2012/10/09/the-social-contract-theory-in-a-global-context/.

15. Riberio, Gustavo Lins. *What is Cosmopolitanism?*. Accessed October 23, 2015. http://www.vibrant.org.br/downloads/v2n1_ wc.pdf.

16. Sickler, Melvin. "A Satanic Plot for a One World Government: The World Conspirators: the Illuminati." *The Forbidden Knowledge*. Last accessed November 27, 2015. http://www.theforbiddenknowledge.com/h ardtruth/satanic_plot_government.htm.

17. Stanford Encyclopedia of Philosophy. "Cosmopolitanism." Accessed October 23, 2015. http://plato.stanford.edu/entries/cosmopoli tanism/.

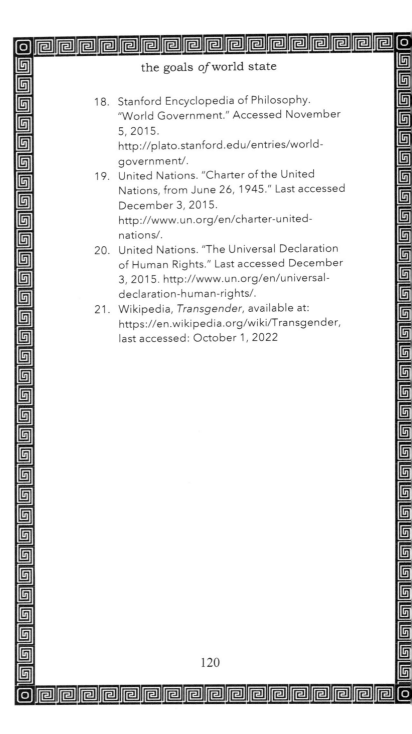

18. Stanford Encyclopedia of Philosophy. "World Government." Accessed November 5, 2015. http://plato.stanford.edu/entries/world-government/.
19. United Nations. "Charter of the United Nations, from June 26, 1945." Last accessed December 3, 2015. http://www.un.org/en/charter-united-nations/.
20. United Nations. "The Universal Declaration of Human Rights." Last accessed December 3, 2015. http://www.un.org/en/universal-declaration-human-rights/.
21. Wikipedia, *Transgender*, available at: https://en.wikipedia.org/wiki/Transgender, last accessed: October 1, 2022

AUTHOR'S NOTE:

Thank you for your time dedicating in reading this short book.

More research:

Black and White Music: A Journey Behind the Musical Notes (2022): In this report I explored a very small part of the music industry from the USA, more precisely, I investigated the contribution, greater or lesser, of black and white artists in the production and writing of their albums. The artists investigated in this report are Taylor Swift, Kanye West, Beyoncé, Kendrick Lamar, Macklemore & Ryan, Adele and Beck. I selected these artists because the music produced and released by them were used by various artists and journalists as examples of racial discrimination that takes place in the music industry.

On the *Famous* Feud (2022): In this report I investigated the feud between Kim Kardashian, Kanye West and Taylor Swift. The mechanisms for interpreting the feud are multiple and there is still a great interest in debating the perpetrators and the victims of the feud. I'm gonna let you finish reading it, but 'On the Famous Feud' is a unique and original investigation, there is no other research that explores this conflict on various levels.

THE FULL EXPERIENCE OF REVI PROJECT 88 IS AVAILABLE ONLINE:

Printed in Poland
by Amazon Fulfillment
Poland Sp. z o.o., Wrocław

17201106R00069